New Edition
Skits
In English

MARY ELIZABETH HINES

Regents Publishing Company, Inc.

Illustrations by Melanie Parsowith

10 9 8 7 6 5 4 3 2 1

Published by
Regents Publishing Company, Inc.
2 Park Avenue
New York, N.Y. 10016

Printed in the United States of America
ISBN 0-88345-372-X

ACKNOWLEDGMENTS

Since the publication of the original *Skits*, I have had the chance to share them with several groups of teachers in the States and overseas. Invariably, questions, observations, and suggestions from participants in workshops led to insights on strengths and weaknesses of the material which, in turn, led to the changes evident in this edition. To teachers who have given warm and generous criticism and to students who let me share their fun, my thanks.

I am equally grateful to my editor, Pam Breyer, whose talents and sense of perfection guided the present text from its manuscript stage to its present form

M.E.H.

CONTENTS

INTRODUCTION

This collection of skits is a revised version of *Skits in English as a Second Language*. As a result of my own experiences since the original collection and in response to suggestions and criticisms made by teachers who have used them, changes have been made. Skits which teachers found confusing to students and some which were considered sexist were removed or edited. In this collection of thirty skits, ten are new. In addition, each skit is now followed by suggested role-playing activities which elicit free use of English by students.

Originally, the skits were intended for adult students at the beginning level. Teachers have informed me, however, that they are using them with beginning and intermediate students at the junior-high-school level and with intermediate and advanced students in courses concerned with pronunciation, stress, and intonation. The content of the skits allows teachers and students to focus on nonverbal gestures, sighs, actions, and the messages of anger, boredom, sarcasm, frustration, humor, and comraderie that varied intonation patterns convey. It has followed that students incidentally memorize the basic pattern each skit focuses on as they repeat idiomatic phrases whose messages are recognizable in context.

It is this establishing of a context that is the chief value of the skits. Language items isolated for study have been put back into a language environment with a conflict of some kind, providing reasons to use them. The series lends itself to supplementing a traditional grammar-oriented syllabus and, at the same time, will be recognized by advocates of a functional syllabus: the skits say that these characters in these situations are likely to say these words. They may or may not be used by all native speakers of English. That is, language is presented in situations that represent real life day-to-day, out-of-class situations. Nuances of word meanings are elicited by noting the problem and personality a given character has. And, while the skits were always meant to enhance communicative competence among students, the speech acts, the functions, inherent in each skit have now been identified and noted. As with any conversational setting, there are usually at least two functions present in any exchange.

These skits are not the dialogues found in most second-language texts—if only because the second half of a contrived dialogue is seldom encountered by students once they leave class. Instead, the skits offer a conflict of some kind and, together with the improvisational activities, expose the students to the unpredictable. They bring into class the pressures students and native speakers of English experience outside of class, for by initiating and responding in class to language that is accompanied by tension, noise, humor, and other distractions, students are better able to initiate and respond to language outside of class.

The rationale behind the skits (beyond providing simple practice material) is that behind all role-playing activities students are presented with a mask. By assuming the persona of another person, the students become safe: it is no longer Student A self-consciously speaking and making mistakes. It is Henry Smith or the waiter. Inhibitions are relieved, and students become more receptive to corrections. In the course of acting, language flows; the students take risks which are not taken in traditional classroom exercises. The skits allow students and teachers to use the psychology of humor, the relaxation, and give-and-take that is inherent in role-playing. In the process of losing self-consciousness, students feel less threatened and speak more freely. At the most elementary level, language can be fun and functional.

Short and Long Answers

Before discussing role-playing activities, a word about Exercise A which follows each skit. Exercise A is a means of demonstrating student comprehension of the skit but, just as important, it is designed to demonstrate the differences between the spoken and written language. It is not meant to be a testing exercise but one which will elicit more spoken language from students. Each question is followed by the usual spoken response, a word or a phrase, not an artificial sentence. But people do not spend their second-language careers responding to questions. At times, they will initiate exchanges with a sentence; other times, they will want to write complete sentences. For this reason, the short answers are followed by complete sentences. The exercise is exploited most effectively if students ask the questions of each other. The students should be encouraged to cover the answer, attempt their own, and then immediately compare their answer with the one given. After comprehension has been confirmed, it is time to turn to the prime purpose of the skits, role-playing.

Suggested Uses

Many variations of the following activities are possible depending on the language ability of the students and the time teachers can spend on acting. Concerning the latter, though, it is often a false economy to move on "to cover" more grammar before students have mastered what was first taught.

But the sequence from control to freedom is presented first. After students have practiced a given structure, say the present continuous tense, turn to the appropriate skit, "After-Dinner Harmony." Before reading the skit, assign a role to every student so that the entire class is involved in the skit from the very beginning. This means that in a class of twenty or thirty (or sixty) there will be three or four Mr. Sullivans who will speak in unison. Making the scene as graphic as possible, whether it be using the illustrations in the text or stick figures on the board, the teacher should model the lines of each character and have students assigned those roles repeat the lines. All students should not recite all lines. Only Mr. Sullivan repeats Mr. Sullivan's lines; in fact, instead of just repeating them, he is to address them to Keith or Lisa or whomever. From the beginning, the teacher is a background voice; the actors speak to each other.

Throughout the skits, new vocabulary has been kept to a minimum. A close reading will often show that words are either defined in accompanying stage directions or in lines following new or abstract expressions. But, after the first reading, using the context of the skit and/or gestures, the teacher should demonstrate the meaning of words unfamiliar to students. After it is clear that students are not hindered by strange words, conduct a second reading with the students holding to their original characters. Once a skit has been introduced, a student should assume one role and not move back and forth mechanically reciting lines. Then, while they are still sitting at their seats, have one group of students read the skit. That is, a cast of Mr. Sullivan, Keith, Lisa, etc., reads the lines while others listen. At this point, students who are not in the performing group can be asked to serve as prompters for students having trouble with lines and as sound effects people supplying the sounds of music, phone ringing, or doorbell ringing.

With most classes, one group of students is usually ready to do a skit stage-fashion after the third reading. They move to the front of the class, and with furniture and space blocked out to represent rooms in a house, the students get ready to perform, using real or simulated props. A hat can be a bowl of soup, for example. In order not to threaten students or lose the fun of acting, teachers should not force students to act in front of the class until they are ready. This fourth reading is usually the appropriate time. This fourth group, however, is asked *not to read or recite* lines but *to mime* the lines and actions of each character. The step calls student attention to gestures and facial expressions they will eventually use along with words. At the same time, it pulls their attention away from words, allowing them *to focus on meaning, not form*. The fifth group of students will perform the skit stage-fashion with lines and actions.

Correcting language problems at this point is important, but it should be done selectively. Unless language is totally unintelligible, the teacher should let the students complete the skit, taking note of pronunciation and intonation problems each character has. When the skit is finished, addressing the student as a character, select only one mistake or one kind of problem so that students can attend to and incorporate the correction. Too many corrections are confusing and cause frustration. After the fifth group has performed, assign the skit for homework and begin the next class with still another group of students performing the skit.

Improvisational Activities

It is helpful to have beginning students experience the pressure of the unpredictable in class and it is at this time, after they demonstrate ease with a skit, that improvisation is valuable. Using the situation and characters of the skit studied, direct students *not* to use the prescribed lines but to say what they want. This activity, by its nature, forces students to listen to each other and respond to each other with acceptable lines, that is, lines that make sense in context. More important, it forces students to think in English.

Let the improvisation last only two or three minutes so teacher and students can remember what was said and, at the end of each segment, make corrections. The most effective way is to tape the exchange, play back the incorrect language, and then have students repeat the correct way. But with most classes where only the students on the tape are interested enough to attend, the most efficient way is to note the incorrect language and then give the correct utterance. For example, if Mr. Sullivan says, "I washing the dishes" that is what the teacher should note; then at the end of the scene, the teacher should model, "I'm washing the dishes" and have the student repeat the phrase or sentence.

In many of the improvisational activities, the students are again asked to be the same characters, but the situation changes to one which relies on the content of the original skit. Following "After-Dinner Harmony," for example, the students are asked to act out what they think takes place at the end of the skit. Other improvisational activities call for the same function in a new situation with new characters and a new conflict. By its nature, this type of exercise elicits expressions using the structure that was highlighted in the skit itself but students have to determine what a character would be like and what he or she is likely to say in this particular situation. It calls for genuine improvisation.

In genuine improvisation, only two or three students perform stage-fashion at a time. But preparation for it can include all students in groups of three or four working on what they would say while the teacher works with individuals who have questions. After a five-minute period of practice, one group can perform in front of the class for a two or three-minute segment. Again, the teacher can correct along the lines suggested earlier. Not all students will necessarily perform all improvisational activities in one class, but in the course of a term each will have had the chance to improvise under pressure.

Whether working with prescribed lines in a skit or experimenting with genuine improvisation, students benefit from role-playing in a class. Relaxation prevents them from trying too hard, a phenomenon which seems to result in more student talk and more correct language. Responding to the unpredictable under friendly pressure leads students to think in English in class which in turn prepares them to use English outside of class. Whether the role-playing is five minutes or fifty minutes in duration, after earlier time spent on drills and exercises, teacher and student, both, experience the pleasure that comes from communicating in a second language.

Mary Hines

"FLY" SOUP

ARGUING; EXPRESSING CURIOSITY
PRESENT TENSE OF *TO BE* WITH *THIS* AND *THAT*

Characters: Henry Smith
A waiter
Customer 1
Customer 2
Customer 3
The restaurant manager

Scene: A crowded New York restaurant

Henry: Waiter. Waiter!

(*The waiter comes up to Henry.*)

Waiter: Yes?

Henry: There's a fly in my soup!

Waiter: That's impossible.

Henry: Look.

Waiter: Where?

Henry: There. What's that? (*He points to a speck in the soup.*)

Waiter: What? (*He leans over to look at the soup.*)

Henry: That little black speck with wings. What's that? (*He points to a fly.*)

Waiter: Black pepper! It's black pepper!

Henry: It is NOT black pepper. It's a fly!

(*The customers crowd around the table.*)

Customer 1: What's wrong?

Customer 2: What's the matter?

1

Customer 3:	What is it?
Henry:	There's a fly in my soup!
Waiter:	He says there's a fly in his soup.
Customer 1:	Where is it?
Customer 2:	Let me see.
Henry:	There.
Customer 1:	Yes, that's a fly.
Customer 2:	No, it isn't.
Henry:	Yes, it is!
Waiter:	No, it ISN'T!
Manager:	(*He runs up to the table.*) What's going on here?
Waiter:	This man says there's a fly in his soup.
Manager:	There's a fly in his soup? In MY restaurant? That's impossible.
Henry:	Here. What's this? Is this a fly or not? (*He picks up a spoonful of soup with a fly in it.*)
Manager:	Shh. Please, mister, shh. Waiter, bring a steak dinner.
Henry:	Well, maybe . . .
Manager:	Bring a steak dinner and wine and pie and coffee.
	(*The waiter leaves. A box falls from Henry's pocket.*)
Customer 1:	What's that?
Customer 2:	What?
Customer 1:	This. (*He picks up the box.*)
Manager:	What is it?
Customer 1:	It's a box of flies!
	(*Henry gets up from the table.*)
Manager:	Get out of my restaurant! Get out! (*He runs after Henry.*)

A. Answer these questions. Use short answers (the usual spoken response) and long answers (for structural practice).

Example: Where is Henry   → In a restaurant.
Smith?   He's in a restaurant.

  1. Where is Henry Smith?   → In a restaurant. He's in a restaurant.

2

2. Where is the restaurant? → In New York. The restaurant is in New York.

3. Are there many people in the restaurant? → Yes, there are. There are many people in the restaurant.

4. Is the restaurant crowded? → Yes, it is. It's crowded.

5. Is there a black speck in Henry's soup? → Yes, there is. There's a black speck in Henry's soup.

6. Is it black pepper or a fly? → A fly. It's a fly.

7. Is the manager embarrassed about the fly in the soup? → Yes, he is. He's embarrassed about the fly in the soup.

8. What falls from Henry's pocket? → A box. A box falls from Henry's pocket.

9. What is in the box? → Flies. Flies are in the box.

10. Is the manager angry? → Yes, he is. He's angry.

B. Improvise

1. What is the conversation between the manager and the other customers after Henry leaves?

2. Peggy and Larry are eating in a restaurant. They find a dirty spoon and call the waiter. What is the conversation?

THE MYSTERIOUS BOX

EXPRESSING CURIOSITY; REPRIMANDING
THE INDEFINITE ARTICLE

Characters: Debbie
Karen
Courtney } second graders
Bill
Jim, a fifth-grade monitor
Jean, a sixth-grade monitor

Scene: It is recess time at Happy Acres Elementary School. The second graders are in their classroom.

Jim: (*He comes into the room with his hands on his hips.*) You're supposed to be in the schoolyard. . . . What's that? What is that noise? (*He points to a box on the floor.*) What is THAT?

Debbie: It's a . . . a . . . It's a . . . (*She laughs and points around the corner.*)

Jim: A what? What is it? (*The box moves. He jumps.*) Is it a spring?

Karen: No, no. It isn't a spring.

Jim: Is it a cat?

Courtney: No, it's not a cat.

(*The box moves again.*)

Jim: A dog? Is it a dog?

Debbie: No, no. It isn't a dog.

Jim: Well, what is it? (*The box jumps. Jim jumps.*) Debbie, is it a rabbit? In the CLASSROOM?

Courtney: No, no, Jim. It isn't a rabbit.

(*The girls giggle. Jean, a sixth-grade monitor, comes into the room.*)

Jean: What is that noise? (*She glares at everyone. The girls freeze.*) What

5

is that box? (*She points to the box. It jumps.*)

Jim: I don't know, Jean.

(*Jean bends over and finds a wire attached to the box.*)

Jean: Aha! What is this? It's a wire! (*She follows the wire around the corner to the cloakroom.*) Bill!

(*Bill, another second grader, comes out of the cloakroom. His face is red.*)

Bill: Uh, hi, Jean.

Jean: Tell me, Bill. WHAT IS THAT?

Bill: A present, Jean. It's a present for everyone.

(*Jean accidentally steps on the wire. The box jumps. Jean jumps. Jim screams. Everyone laughs. Bill groans.*)

Jim: What is it? What IS it?

Jean: Bill, open that box!

Bill: OK. (*Under the box is a rubber mouse. Jim jumps.*) It's a mouse, Jean. (*Jean screams.*) It isn't a real mouse. It's a toy.

Jean: A mouse, huh? It's a toy, huh? Well, Bill, and you others, this is a SCHOOL. (*She waves at the room.*)

Bill: Yes, Jean.

Jean: It is NOT a circus.

Bill: Yes, Jean.

Jean: It is NOT a toy shop.

Girls, Bill: Yes, Jean.

(*Jean walks away.*)

Jim: Remember, you kids. This is a SCHOOL. It is NOT a circus!

(*The second graders collapse with laughter.*)

A. Answer these questions. Use short answers (the usual spoken response) and long answers (for structural practice).

Example: Where are the children?	→ In their classroom. They're in their classroom.
1. Where are the children?	→ In their classroom. They're in their classroom.
2. What time is it?	→ Recess. It's recess (time).

6

3. Who are Debbie, Karen and Courtney? → Second graders. They're second graders.

4. Who is Bill? → Another second grader. He's a second grader.

5. Who is Jim? → A fifth-grade monitor. He's a fifth-grade monitor.

6. Who is Jean? → A sixth-grade monitor. She's a sixth-grade monitor.

7. Why is Jim angry at the second graders? → Because they're noisy. He's angry because the second graders are noisy.

8. What is on the floor? → A box. There's a box on the floor.

9. Is there a real animal in the box? → No, there isn't. There isn't a real animal in the box.

10. What is in the box? → A toy mouse. There's a toy mouse in the box.

B. Improvise

1. What do the second graders say after Jim and Jean leave?

2. People are in the savings account line in a bank. The line is very slow and everyone is impatient. A young man enters the bank and goes right to the window for service. What do the other customers say to the young man?

AFTER-DINNER HARMONY

MAKING EXCUSES
PRESENT CONTINUOUS TENSE WITH DIRECT OBJECTS

Characters: Mr. Sullivan
Keith Sullivan, age nineteen
Lisa Sullivan, age fourteen
Dick Sullivan ⎫
Tom Sullivan ⎭ twins, age twelve
John Sullivan, age eight
Jeff, Keith's friend

Scene: It is after dinner in the Sullivan house. Mrs. Sullivan is away on a trip. Keith, home on vacation from college, is in the study. He's writing a term paper. Mr. Sullivan is in the kitchen. Lisa, Tom, Dick, and John are all upstairs.

(*from upstairs*) Bang! Bang! Bang!

Keith: Dad? Dad?

Mr. Sullivan: (*from the kitchen*) What is it? I'm washing the dishes.

Keith: Who's making that noise? I'm writing a term paper.

(*Mr. Sullivan walks to the foot of the stairs.*)

Mr. Sullivan: John? What's that noise you're making? Your brother is writing a term paper.

John: Gee whiz, Dad. I'm building a rocket for school. I'm showing it in science class tomorrow.

Mr. Sullivan: Keith, John is building a rocket for his science class. (*He returns to the kitchen.*)

Keith: Well, I'm trying to write this term paper.

(*The phone rings.*)

9

Mr. Sullivan:	Oh, darn it. The phone is ringing. Lisa! Lisa? Please answer the telephone. I'm washing the dishes.
Lisa:	(*from the bathroom*) What? What?
Mr. Sullivan:	Please answer the telephone. I'm washing the dishes.
Lisa:	(*She yells from the bathroom.*) But Dad, I'm washing my hair. Tell Clifford I'll call him later.
Mr. Sullivan:	Dick? Tom? The telephone is ringing. Where are the twins? DICK? TOM? The telephone is ringing!
Dick:	(*from upstairs*) I'm studying. Tom's watching TV.
Tom:	I'm watching the baseball game, Dad.
Mr. Sullivan:	Well, I'M washing the dishes, so SOMEONE ANSWER THE TELEPHONE!!
	(*Keith walks to the phone in the hallway.*)
Keith:	No, no, this isn't 567-4092. This is 567-4093.
Lisa:	(*from upstairs*) Is that Clifford calling?
Keith:	No. Wrong number. (*He returns to the study.*) And I'm STILL trying to write my term paper. (*loud music from upstairs*) Oh, no! Hey, Dad? What's going on NOW?
Mr. Sullivan:	It's music. Lisa? What are you doing?
Lisa:	I'm drying my hair, Dad.
Dick:	She's dancing, Dad. She's dancing! She's drying her hair and dancing. The whole house is shaking and I'm trying to study.
Lisa:	I'm drying my hair and listening to a new disco record. (*The doorbell rings.*) Oh, the doorbell's ringing. I bet it's Clifford! (*She runs to the top of the stairs and yells down.*) Tell Clifford I'm hurrying! (*She runs back to her room.*)
John:	(*He yells from upstairs.*) Hey, Dad? The twins are fighting.
Mr. Sullivan:	Tom, Dick, what are you doing?
Dick:	I'm studying for a test, Dad. But Tom's watching TV and listening to the radio at the same time.
Tom:	I'm NOT listening to the radio, Dad. I'm watching the baseball game.
Mr. Sullivan:	Is the radio on?
Tom:	Yes, but . . .
Mr. Sullivan:	No radio and no baseball game while Dick is studying.
Tom:	Aw, Dad.

(*The doorbell rings again.*)

Lisa: (*yelling*) Isn't anyone going to answer the door?

Mr. Sullivan: And Lisa, NO disco music.

Lisa: Well, I'm going out anyway. (*yelling*) Tell Clifford I'm coming!

(*Keith answers the door.*)

Keith: Hi, Jeff!

Jeff: Hey, Keith. Can I work on my term paper here? Our house is so noisy. My kid brothers are watching the baseball game, playing the piano, and building a bookcase.

(*There is a huge crash from upstairs.*)

John: (*yelling*) Hey, the rocket's taking off! My rocket's exploding!!

Mr. Sullivan: Why don't you guys go to the library?

Keith: Jeff, let's go to the library.

A. Answer these questions. Use both short and long answers.

Example: What is Mr. Sullivan doing? → Washing the dishes.
He's washing the dishes.

1. What is Mr. Sullivan doing? → Washing the dishes. He's washing the dishes.

2. What is Keith doing? → Writing a term paper. He's writing a term paper.

3. What is John doing? → Building a rocket. He's building a rocket.

4. Is the phone ringing? → Yes, it is. The phone is ringing.

5. What is Lisa doing? → Washing her hair. She's washing her hair.

6. What is Dick doing? → Studying. He's studying.

7. What is Tom doing? → Watching TV. He's watching TV.

8. Is Lisa listening to disco music? → Yes, she is. She's listening to disco music.

9. Are the twins fighting? → Yes, they are. The twins are fighting.

10. Is the Sullivan house quiet? → No, it isn't. It isn't quiet.

B. Improvise

1. What is the conversation in the Sullivan house after Keith and Jeff leave?

2. After breakfast on a Saturday morning, Mrs. Blatchford wants to go to the park. Mr. Blatchford wants to stay home. They have a two-year-old son. What is the conversation?

11

THE SIDEWALKS OF NEW YORK

INQUIRING; AVOIDING ANSWERS
PRESENT CONTINUOUS TENSE WITH DIRECT OBJECTS

Characters: Sam, a man from the neighborhood   A teen-age boy
Dan   A teen-age girl
Mike   } strangers   A police officer
Marge, a waitress

Scene: A street in New York City at midnight. Two strangers, Dan and Mike, are digging a hole in the sidewalk. Sam is taking his dog for a walk.

Sam: What are you doing? (*He looks down at Dan and Mike. They continue digging.*)

Dan: What?

Sam: What are you doing?

Dan: What do you mean, "What are you doing?"

Mike: What do you THINK we're doing?

Dan: What are YOU doing?

Sam: I'M walking my dog. YOU'RE digging a hole in the middle of the sidewalk.

Mike: That's right, mister. We're digging a hole in the middle of the sidewalk.

Sam: Why?

Dan: Huh?

Sam: Why are you digging a hole in the middle of the sidewalk in the middle of the night?

Mike: Why are you standing there in the middle of the sidewalk in the middle of the night? And why are you asking questions?

(*Marge walks by. She is coming home from work.*)

Marge:	(*to Sam*) What are you doing?
Sam:	I'm watching them.
Marge:	What are they doing?
Sam:	I don't know. Ask them.
Marge:	(*to Mike and Dan*) Hello! What are you doing?
Dan:	Lady, please. What do you think we're doing?
Marge:	You're digging a hole.
Dan:	That's right.
Mike:	Lady, you're very smart!
Marge:	And YOU'RE very rude!
Mike:	Hey, Dan, we're very rude! (*They laugh.*)
	(*A teen-age boy and girl come along. They are holding hands.*)
Boy:	Hey, man, what's happening?
Marge:	Two rude men are digging a hole.
Girl:	Oh! (*to the men*) What are you doing?
Mike:	Dan?
Dan:	Yeah?
Mike:	What are we doing?
Dan:	We're digging a hole.
Mike:	We're taking dirt from the ground with shovels.
Dan:	That's right.
Mike:	So why are they asking us stupid questions?
Marge:	(*to the others*) See? Aren't they rude?
Boy:	Hey, man, are you digging a hole for Public Works?
Mike:	No, mister, we're NOT digging a hole for Public Works.
Sam:	I know. You're digging a hole for the Water Department!
Dan:	. . . And we're NOT digging a hole for the Water Department!!
	(*A police officer arrives. He is swinging his nightstick.*)
Police Officer:	OK. OK. What's happening? Why are you all standing here?
Girl:	We're watching them. They're digging a hole.
Marge:	And they're very rude, officer.
Police Officer:	Hey, down there. What are you doing?
Dan:	What? (*then quietly, to Mike*) Hey, it's the cops.

Police Officer:	Are you digging a hole for Public Works?
Marge:	Oh, no, officer. They're not digging a hole for Public Works.
Police Officer:	Are you digging a hole for the Water Department?
Sam:	No, they're not digging a hole for the Water Department.
Police Officer:	Oh! (*He walks toward a police call box.*)
Girl:	Officer, what are you doing?
Police Officer:	I'm calling a patrol car.
Boy:	Why?
Police Officer:	Because they're digging a hole under the Blair National Bank, THAT'S why!!

A. Answer these questions. Remember, when possible use both short and long answers.

1. What time is it? → Midnight. It's midnight.

2. Is Sam in New York City or in Boston? → New York City. He's in New York City.

3. What is Sam doing? → Taking a walk. He's taking his dog for a walk.

4. What are Mike and Dan doing? → Digging a hole. They're digging a hole.

5. What is Marge doing? → Walking home from work. She's walking home from work.

6. What are the teen-agers doing? → Holding hands. They're holding hands.

7. Are Mike and Dan digging a hole for Public Works? → No, they're not. They're not digging a hole for Public Works.

8. Are Mike and Dan digging a hole for the Water Department? → No, they're not. They're not digging a hole for the Water Department.

9. Where are Mike and Dan digging a hole? → Under the Blair National Bank. They're digging a hole under the Blair National Bank.

10. Why are they digging a hole under the Blair National Bank? → To rob the Blair National Bank. They're robbing the Blair National Bank.

B. Improvise

1. Mike and Dan are running away as the police officer calls for a patrol car. What is their conversation?

2. Barry calls Laura to ask her to a soccer game. Laura is very busy. What is the phone conversation?

WHOSE PARTY?

EXPRESSING DISPLEASURE; AVOIDING BLAME
POSSESSIVE ADJECTIVES AND POSSESSIVE PRONOUNS

Characters: Mr. Henry, fifty years old
Mrs. Henry, forty-five years old
Jerry, their fifteen-year-old son
Susan, their seventeen-year-old daughter
Derek, their seventeen-year-old nephew
Nancy, their sixteen-year-old neighbor

Scene: The Henrys' living room. Jerry and Susan are having a party. Mr. and Mrs. Henry come home early from a vacation. When they enter the front door, twenty teen-agers run out the back door. Nancy and Derek jump behind the sofa and hide. Jerry and Susan stand in the middle of the room.

Mr. Henry: What's going on here? Come back here! (*He turns to Jerry and Susan.*) Who was here? (*They don't reply.*) OK, then. WHOSE JACKET is this?

Jerry: Uh, Derek's. It's Derek's jacket, Dad.

Derek: (*whispering to Nancy behind the sofa*) That's not my jacket. It's David's jacket.

Nancy: Shh.

Mrs. Henry: CIGARETTES! (*She picks up a pack of cigarettes from the table.*) Whose cigarettes are these?

Susan: (*She glances at Jerry.*) I think they're. . . .

Jerry: (*interrupting*) No, they're not. They're Derek's cigarettes.

Derek: (*whispering indignantly*) Mine? They're not mine! They're HIS. (*He hits his head as he tries to get up.*)

Nancy: Shh!

Mr. Henry: So Derek was here. Your cousin. And who else was here?

17

(Susan and Jerry don't answer.)

Mrs. Henry: *(picking up a sweater from a chair)* Here's Nancy's sweater. Nancy was here. *(She looks at Susan.)*

Susan: Yes, that's her sweater.

Nancy: *(whispering to Derek)* And she's my friend.

Mrs. Henry: And this? What's THIS? *(She picks up a beer can.)*

Mr. Henry: It's a BEER CAN. In MY house. With MY son and daughter! *(He glares at his son.)* WHOSE BEER IS THIS?

Jerry: I don't know. *(He tries to change the subject.)* These are John's records and Mimi's stereo and . . . *(Susan kicks him in the foot.)*

Mr. Henry: What's a beer can doing in my house?

Mrs. Henry: And what is Mimi's stereo doing in our house on a school night? Whose party was this?

Jerry: It was our party. *(Susan kicks him again.)* I mean, it was Derek's party.

Derek: *(muttering furiously)* It was YOUR party! *(He tries to get up. Nancy grabs him. He hits his head again.)*

Mr. Henry: *(very sweetly)* So . . . it was Derek's party. *(shouting)* And why was Derek having a party in MY HOUSE?

Jerry: It was our party.

Mr. Henry: Without our permission!

Susan: Dad, please. It was a surprise party for Derek's birthday.

Derek: *(grumbling behind the couch)* Some cousin. Some birthday.

Susan: Dad! What are you doing?

Mr. Henry: I'm calling Derek's father about Derek's beer and Derek's cigarettes in my house.

Jerry: *(pleadingly)* But it was Derek's birthday, Dad.

Mrs. Henry: And about Derek's birthday party, in our house on a school night without our permission!

(Susan and Jerry groan.)

Mr. Henry: Whose feet are these? *(He points to Derek's feet.)*

Mrs. Henry: *(pointing to Nancy's fingers)* And whose hands are those?

(Nancy and Derek stand up.)

Nancy: Oh, hello Mr. and Mrs. Henry. I . . . uh . . . just want to thank you for the really nice party.

Derek: Uh, yeah! Right! Thanks for the party! We have to go now. Bye!

(*Derek and Nancy run out the front door.*)

Mr. Henry: COME BACK HERE!

A. Answer these questions. Use both short and long answers.

1. Who comes home early from vacation?
→ Mr. and Mrs. Henry. Mr. and Mrs. Henry come home early from vacation.

2. What is going on in the Henry house?
→ A party. There's a party going on in the Henry house.

3. Who runs out the back door?
→ Twenty teen-agers. Twenty teen-agers run out the back door.

4. Who is standing in the living room?
→ Susan and Jerry. Susan and Jerry are standing in the living room.

5. Who is hiding behind the couch?
→ Derek and Nancy. Derek and Nancy are hiding behind the couch.

6. Whose jacket is on the sofa?
→ David's. David's jacket is on the sofa.

7. Whose sweater is on the chair?
→ Nancy's. Nancy's sweater is on the chair.

8. Whose records are in the house?
→ John's. John's records are in the house.

9. Whose stereo is in the house?
→ Mimi's. Mimi's stereo is in the house.

10. Whose father is Mr. Henry calling?
→ Derek's father. Mr. Henry is calling Derek's father.

B. Improvise

1. What is the conversation between Derek and Nancy on the way home?

2. What is the conversation between Derek and Jerry when they meet the next day?

A "HAPPY" AUDIENCE

LOCATING SEATS IN A THEATER; COMPLAINING
POSSESSIVE ADJECTIVES AND POSSESSIVE PRONOUNS

Characters: Agnes and Mabel, two elderly sisters
Vincent and Linda, two theater-lovers
Sid and Janet, sitting in the audience behind Vincent and Linda
The usher
Members of the audience

Scene: A dark theater

Agnes: (*whispering*) Mabel, someone's in our seats.

Mabel: *(She is hard of hearing.)* What, dear?

Agnes: Someone is sitting in our seats. See? (*She points to Vincent and Linda.*)

Sid and Janet: Shhhh.

Mabel: Oh, yes. *(She speaks aloud to Vincent and Linda.)* Excuse me. You're sitting in our seats.

Vincent: Pardon me, ladies. But we're not sitting in your seats. They're ours.

Agnes: Mabel, dear, that man is sitting in my seat!

Sid: Please be quiet!

Mabel: (*to Agnes in a loud voice*) Hush, dear. (*to Vincent*) I'm sorry, but they're not your seats. My ticket is for Seat 101. My sister's is for Seat 102. You're sitting in 101 and 102.

(*Vincent looks for his tickets.*)

Sid: (*to Janet*) Why don't people look at their tickets and find their seats BEFORE the show?

Vincent: (*He glares at Sid and then stands up to catch the light while he looks at his tickets. Sid and Janet groan.*) I'm sorry, but OUR tickets are for seats 102 and 101. These are our seats. (*He sits down.*)

21

Agnes: Mabel, those are not their seats. They're OUR seats.

Sid: Ladies, ladies! Please talk to the usher!

Mabel: Where is the usher?

Agnes: Yes, where is the usher?

Usher: (*He comes down the aisle with a flashlight.*) What is it?

People: Shhhh!

Mabel: They're sitting in our seats!

Usher: Where are your tickets, madam?

Mabel: Here's mine. And this is my sister's.

People: Shhhhhh!

Agnes: My seat is 102. Hers is 101.

Mabel: (*to Agnes*) Hush, dear.

Usher: (*to Vincent*) Sir, may I see your ticket?

Vincent: These are our seats.

Usher: But where is your ticket?

Vincent: Here.

Usher: And the lady's ticket?

Vincent: Here!

People: Shhhh!

Sid: (*to the usher*) Hey, mister, please hurry up and find their seats.

Usher: (*to Vincent*) Sorry, sir. You're in the wrong seats. Your tickets are 101 and 102 in Row E. These seats are 101 and 102 in Row D.

Vincent: Well, who's sitting in MY seat? (*He turns and glares at Sid.*) Look at HIS ticket.

People: Groan. Please! Shhhhhh!

Usher: May I please see your ticket?

Sid: Here.

Usher: Your ticket is for Row F. You're sitting in Row E.

People: Shhhhhhh!

Agnes: Mabel, dear, I told you someone was sitting in our seats.

Mabel: Hush, dear.

A. Answer these questions. Use both short and long answers.

1. Where are Agnes and Mabel? → At the theater. They're at the theater.

2. Are they early or late? → Late. They're late.

3. What are they doing? → Looking for their seats. They're looking for their seats.

4. Why are they whispering? → They're late. They're late and people are watching the play.

5. Who is sitting in Agnes and Mabel's seats? → Vincent and Linda. Vincent and Linda are sitting in their seats.

6. What seats are Vincent and Linda sitting in? → 101 and 102 in Row D. They're sitting in 101 and 102 in Row D.

7. Are Vincent and Linda in the right seats? → No, they're not. They're not in the right seats.

8. What seats are their tickets for? → 101 and 102 in Row E. Their tickets are for 101 and 102 in Row E.

9. Is Sid angry? → Yes, he is. He's angry.

10. Is there confusion about the tickets? → Yes, there is. There's confusion about the tickets.

B. Improvise

1. Two children get on a crowded bus together. There is one empty seat. They both try to get it. What is the conversation?

2. Mr. and Mrs. Coughlan and Mr. and Mrs. Bruce, strangers, are at an open market looking at rugs. The Coughlans are ready to buy a rug when Mr. Bruce picks the rug up and tells the rug dealer he wants it. What is the conversation?

MYSTERY HOUSE

EXPRESSING FEAR; SURPRISING SOMEONE
THERE IS

Characters: Richard Erickson
Ruth Erickson
Stephanie Powers
Marvin Powers

Scene: Outside a house on a dark suburban street. The Ericksons are returning home after dinner with their friends, Stephanie and Marvin Powers.

Richard: There's some really good cake left, isn't there, Ruth?

Ruth: Yes, there is. And there's some pie. (*She and Stephanie stop at the front door.*) Shhh.

Stephanie: What is it? Is there anything wrong?

Ruth: Yes, there's something wrong. Shhh!

Stephanie: What?

Ruth: There's something strange about the house.

(*Stephanie moves closer to Marvin.*)

Stephanie: There is?

Marvin: There's nothing wrong. Come on. (*He moves to the door.*)

Richard: Ruth, do you want the keys? (*He starts to get his keys out.*)

Ruth: Wait!

Marvin: (*Stephanie grabs Marvin's arm.*) What is it?

Stephanie: Marvin, maybe there IS something strange.

Ruth: There's something wrong. Shhhh. Listen.

Marvin: Ruth, stop fooling around. There's NOTHING wrong.

Ruth:	Yes, there is!
Richard:	Hey, look. There's a strange car across the street. (*He points across the street.*)
Stephanie:	Marvin, there's someone in the car.
Ruth:	Wait. There's a shadow in the window. (*She points to the window.*)
Marvin:	There isn't any shadow in the window. (*He goes toward the window.*)
Richard:	Yes, there IS! Look! (*He points to the window.*)
Marvin:	(*speaking bravely*) There's also a tree in front of the house, and there's a wind tonight.
Richard:	There IS something strange.
Ruth:	Richard, I'm afraid.
Stephanie:	I'm afraid too. Marvin, where are you?
Marvin:	I'm right here. Relax. There's nothing wrong.
Richard:	Here's the key. Wait a minute. (*He unlocks the door.*) OK, let's go. (*He enters the house. The others follow.*)
Stephanie:	Where are the lights?
Ruth:	There's someone in this room.
Marvin:	There's no one in this room. Ruth! Richard! Where are the lights?
Richard:	The lights are in the living room. (*He and Marvin head toward the living room.*)
Marvin:	(*He trips.*) OUCH!
Ruth:	Be careful! There's a step up.
Marvin:	I know. There's a bruise on my knee to prove it.
	(*Richard flicks the light switch in the living room. There are no lights.*)
Richard:	Ruth, there's something wrong with the lights.
Ruth:	There's a fuse box in the kitchen. (*She and Richard head for the kitchen.*)
Stephanie:	Marvin, there's no light. I'm afraid!
Marvin:	Hey! There's a flashlight in the car. (*He heads for the door.*)
Stephanie:	EEEEECK! (*She screams.*) MAAAARVIN. . . .
Marvin:	Stephanie! . . .
Stephanie:	Marvin? Don't leave me!

Marvin: I'm here. I'm here. (*calling*) Ruth? Richard, is there ANY light? There's something wrong. There's someone in this ROOM!

Stephanie: Marvin.

Richard, Ruth Group: SURPRISE! HAPPY ANNIVERSARY!

(*The lights go on. The room is crowded with friends ready for a party.*)

A. Answer these questions. Remember, when possible use both short and long answers.

1. What are Ruth and Richard doing?
   → Returning home. They're returning home after dinner with their friends, Stephanie and Marvin.

2. Is it dark outside?
   → Yes, it is. It's dark outside.

3. Is there anything wrong?
   → Yes, there is. There's something strange about the house.

4. Is there a strange car across street?
   → Yes, there is. There's a strange car across the street.

5. Is there a shadow in the window?
   → Yes, there is. There's a shadow in the window.

6. Inside the house, is Stephanie afraid?
   → Yes, she is. Stephanie is afraid.

7. Why is she afraid?
   → Because the house is dark. The house is dark and people are in the house.

8. Are the people friends or enemies?
   → Friends. They're friends.

9. Why are people in the house?
   → For a surprise party. Friends are there for a surprise party.

10. What is the party for?
    → Marvin and Stephanie's anniversary. It's a surprise party for Marvin and Stephanie's anniversary.

B. Improvise

1. You are walking in the woods with a friend. It's a pleasant day but the woods are dark. You hear a sound and grab your friend. You hear other sounds. You see shadows. Something moves. What do you and your friend say to each other?

2. An airline has lost your luggage. The airline representative wants a description of the contents of the suitcase. You are very upset. What is the conversation?

HOW MANY MINUTES ARE LEFT?

EXPRESSING BOREDOM; INTERROGATING
THERE ARE; HOW MANY

Characters: Mr. Stevens, a second-grade teacher
Stuart
Thomas
Virginia   second graders
Al
Paul
Joan

Scene: A second-grade classroom

Mr. Stevens: Stuart, how many quarters are there in a dollar? (*Stuart is reading a book.*) Stuart, how many quarters are there in a dollar? Stuart? Stuart!

Stuart: (*He jumps up in a daze.*) What?

Thomas: (*He whispers to Stuart.*) There are five.

Stuart: There are five, Mr. Stevens.

Mr. Stevens: No, no, there are NOT five quarters in a dollar. Sit down. (*Stuart sits down and makes a face at Thomas.*) Virginia?

Virginia: (*She smiles and jumps up quickly.*) There are four quarters in a dollar.

Mr. Stevens: Very good, Virginia. (*Stuart hits Virginia with a pencil and goes back to his book.*) Now, Al, how many minutes are there in an hour?

Al: (*He stands up and recites.*) There are sixty minutes in an hour.

Mr. Stevens: That's right. There are sixty minutes in an hour. Stuart? How many minutes are there in an hour? Stuart???

Stuart: (*He jumps up trying to remember the question.*) Six . . . ? Sixty . . . ? Sixteen . . . ? (*He takes a chance.*) There are sixteen, Mr. Stevens.

Mr. Stevens: There are sixteen whats, Stuart?

Stuart:	I don't know.
Mr. Stevens:	Well, Stuart, there are NOT sixteen minutes in an hour. Now, sit down and LISTEN. (*Stuart sits down and glares.*) Virginia, how many minutes are there in an hour?
Virginia:	(*She jumps up quickly.*) There are sixty minutes in an hour.
Mr. Stevens:	Thank you, Virginia. Now, Thomas, how many days are there in a week?
Thomas:	(*He stands up slowly.*) There are seven days in a week.
Virginia:	(*She jumps up.*) They are Sunday, Monday, Tuesday . . .
Mr. Stevens:	Not now, Virginia.
Virginia:	(*Thomas throws an eraser at Virginia.*) Ouch!
Mr. Stevens:	Is there anything wrong, Virginia?
Virginia:	No, Mr. Stevens. There's nothing wrong.
	(*Virginia kicks Thomas.*)
Mr. Stevens:	There are seven days in a week. How many weeks are there in a month? Paul?
Paul:	(*He gets up and yawns.*) Four. There are four weeks in a month.
Mr. Stevens:	That's right. There are four weeks in a month.
Stuart:	Usually. (*He is doodling at his desk.*)
Mr. Stevens:	Stuart?
Stuart:	Usually there are four weeks in a month. Sometimes there are five.
Mr. Stevens:	That's right, but don't be difficult. USUALLY there are four weeks in a month. How many months in a year? Joan?
Joan:	There are twelve months in a year.
Stuart:	(*He whispers.*) There are nine months in a school year.
Mr. Stevens:	Very good, Joan.
Stuart:	There are three months of vacation.
Virginia:	Mr. Stevens, Stuart is . . . (*Thomas pulls her hair.*) Ouch!
Mr. Stevens:	Is there anything wrong, Virginia?
Virginia:	No, Mr. Stevens, there's nothing wrong.
Mr. Stevens:	Are there any questions? (*silence*) Good. Now . . .
	(*The school bell rings and the students rush out of the classroom.*)

Stuart: There are five school days in a week. There are five hours in a school day. There is one hour for lunch. And there's only ONE Mr. Stevens—and we've got him!

A. Answer these questions. Use both short and long answers.

1. Is Virginia a good student? → Yes, she is. She's a good student.

2. Is Mr. Stevens a good teacher? → No, he isn't. He isn't a good teacher.

3. Is Stuart happy? → No, he isn't. He isn't happy.

4. Is Stuart unintelligent? → No, he isn't. He isn't unintelligent.

5. Is Stuart bored? → Yes, he is. He's bored.

6. How many quarters are there in a dollar? → Four. There are four quarters in a dollar.

7. How many minutes are there in an hour? → Sixty. There are sixty minutes in an hour.

8. How many days are there in a week? → Seven. There are seven days in a week.

9. How many weeks are there in a month? → Four. There are four weeks in a month.

10. How many months are there in a year? → Twelve. There are twelve months in a year.

B. Improvise

1. What is the second graders' conversation during lunch?

2. Rosemary Bertini is moving from one apartment to another. She is trying to get her friend Ralph to help her. Ralph does not want to help her. He does not have much time. He wants to know how many things he must move. What is the conversation?

CAUGHT IN THE ACT

REPROACHING; MAKING EXCUSES

WAS AND *WERE*

Characters: Joanne
Mary
Jack ⎫ high school sophomores
Nat
George ⎭
Nick, a high school senior and star quarterback of the school

Scene: A high school cafeteria at lunch time

Joanne: (*very excited*) Mary, Mary! Guess where *I* was last night!

Mary: Where were you?

Joanne: *I* was at the movies with . . . (*Suddenly she sees Jack and his friends coming.*) Oooops. I'm in trouble.

Mary: What's wrong?

Joanne: I was . . . Oh, Mary, help me.

(*Jack, Nat, and George walk up to the girls. Jack is hurt and angry. Nat and George glare at Joanne.*)

Jack: Where were YOU last night?

Joanne: Jack, I'm so sorry. I tried to call you. I was at the Sports Club. I was in a meeting about . . . (*Jack slams his tray down on the counter.*) What's wrong?

Nat: (*He steps forward.*) You were NOT at the Sports Club last night.

Mary: Yes, she was. (*Mary stands in front of Joanne.*)

Nat: No, she wasn't. *I* was at the Sports Club last night. The doors were shut. The lights were out. It was dark. No one was there.

Mary: Oh! Er, . . . Jo? (*She turns to Joanne.*) Weren't you at the library?

Joanne: That's right! A book was due this morning and . . . (*Jack turns away.*) What's wrong?

George: (*He steps forward.*) Sally and I were at the library last night. YOU certainly weren't there.

Joanne: But when were you there? I was there at seven o'clock and then, then . . . uh . . . I was at Susan's. There was a good show on television. The astronauts were . . . (*Jack turns around and throws his books on the floor.*) What's wrong?

Jack: Nat was at the Sports Club last night until eight o'clock. George and Sally were at the library until nine. Then they all went to Susan's. Only I was home . . . alone! I WAS going to ask you out Saturday. But now . . . (*He picks up his books.*)

Mary: (*whispering to Joanne*) Oh, yes, Jo. You were right. You ARE in trouble.

(*Just then, Nick, a senior and a star quarterback for the school, walks up.*)

Everyone: Hi, Nick.

Nick: Hi there, everybody.

Joanne: (*smiling*) Hi, Nick!

Nick: Hi, Jo! Say, that was a good movie last night. I really liked it. But sorry about Saturday. I can't go. I have another date. (*He leaves.*)

Joanne: Jack?

Jack: Oh, sorry about Saturday, Joanne. I can't go either. I have another date.

(*Jack and the boys leave.*)

Joanne: Jack?

A. Answer these questions. Remember, when possible use both short and long answers.

1. Who are Joanne and Mary? → High school sophomores. They're high school sophomores.

2. Who is in trouble? → Joanne. Joanne is in trouble.

3. Was Joanne at the Sports Club last night? → No, she wasn't. She wasn't at the Sports Club last night.

4. Who was at the Sports Club last night? → Nat. Nat was at the Sports Club last night.

5. Was Joanne at the library last night? → No, she wasn't. She wasn't at the library last night.

34

6. Who was at the library last night?

→ Sally and George. Sally and George were at the library last night.

7. Was Joanne at Susan's house last night?

→ No, she wasn't. She wasn't at Susan's house last night.

8. Who was at Susan's last night?

→ Nat, George, and Sally. Nat, George, and Sally were at Susan's last night.

9. Why is Joanne in trouble?

→ She was at the movies with Nick.

10. Who was home alone last night?

→ Jack. Jack was home alone last night.

B. Improvise

1. What is the conversation between Jack and Nick outside the cafeteria?

2. You took a day off from work yesterday. You told the boss you were home, sick, but he called you and you weren't there. What is the conversation when you return to work?

AUTUMN LEAVES

HINTING

SIMPLE PRESENT

Characters: Ben Woods
Wayne Jones ⎱ teen-agers
Howard Ringer ⎰
Mr. Jones, Wayne's father
Mr. Ringer, Howard's father

Scene: Ben's backyard on a Saturday morning. It is fall. Ben is raking leaves.

Ben: I love the fall. I love the aroma of burning leaves. (*He rakes.*)

Wayne: Autumn means work . . . I love the aroma of apple pie. (*He looks toward the house.*) Hmm. Is your mother baking?

Ben: My father. Every October my father burns leaves and bakes apple pies. I clean up . . . (*He sweeps the back steps.*)

Howard: My father doesn't cook. (*He sighs.*) That pie sure smells good.

Mr. Jones: (*from across the fence*) Wayne, come and put these in a bag.

Wayne: (*groan*) He rakes and shovels and rakes and shovels. Then I haul it all away.

Mr. Jones: Wayne!

Wayne: Coming! Does your father bake a lot? (*He throws a football to Howard.*)

Ben: Not much. Just pies. (*He puts the leaves in a pile.*)

Wayne: Does he make pies often?

Ben: Not often. Apple pies in the fall.

Howard: How many pies does he make? (*He catches the ball and throws it to Wayne.*)

Ben: A lot.

Mr. Jones: Wayne! I need help with the windows!

37

Wayne: I'm coming, Dad. (*He sighs.*) Every year my father takes down screens and puts up storm windows. (*He throws the ball to Howard.*)

Howard: Mine, too. But MY father doesn't want my help. He says I get in the way. Catch! (*He throws the ball to Ben.*)

Mr. Ringer: Howie!

Howard: Oops. Usually.

Ben: (*He catches the ball and throws it back.*) Later, guys.

Wayne: Every Saturday my father washes the car and then waxes it. Really, I wash it and polish it and my father directs.

Ben: You play football every Saturday! (*He picks up some leaves.*) Who are you kidding?

Wayne: Football's more fun. . . . That pie sure smells good.

Howard: I like apple pie.

Ben: Howard, your father is calling you. Wayne, your father . . .

Howard: I know. . . . How long does it take to bake a pie?

Ben: Not long. But my father usually makes several. It takes time.

Wayne: Where do you get the apples?

Ben: In the country.

Howard: Apple pie is nice on a cold day.

Wayne: I wish someone in my family baked.

Howard: Me too . . . I like homemade pie.

Wayne: I never get homemade pie. My folks buy them.

(*They ease up the back stairs to the door.*)

Howard: Does your father need any help?

Ben: I don't think so. (*Mr. Jones comes around the corner.*) Hi, Mr. Jones.

Mr. Jones: There's my son! Wayne, Ben's father has a present for us. I'm here to eat fresh, homemade pie.

(*Mr. Ringer comes around the corner.*)

Mr. Ringer: Is he finished?

Mr. Jones: Yep. He called me. Now, the question is, do we let our hard-working sons join us for the party?

(*Wayne and Howard open their mouths in surprise. Ben laughs as his father opens the kitchen door to let people in.*)

38

A. Answer these questions. Use both short and long answers.

1. What does Ben like in the fall? → The aroma of burning leaves. He loves the aroma of burning leaves.

2. What does Wayne like in the fall? → The aroma of apple pie. He loves the aroma of apple pie.

3. What does Ben's father do every October? → Burn leaves and bake apple pie. He burns leaves and bakes apple pie.

4. Does Howard's father cook? → No, he doesn't. Howard's father doesn't cook.

5. What does Wayne's father do every fall? → Rake and shovel leaves. He rakes and shovels leaves.

6. What does Wayne's father do every Saturday? → Wash and wax the car. He washes and waxes the car.

7. What does Wayne do every Saturday? → Play football. Wayne plays football every Saturday.

8. Do Wayne and Howard help their fathers? → No, they don't. They don't help their fathers.

9. What are Wayne and Howard hoping for? → Apple pie. They're hoping for some apple pie.

10. Do Wayne and Howard get some apple pie? → Yes, they do. They get some apple pie.

B. Improvise

1. What is the conversation between Wayne and Howard and their fathers as they eat the apple pie?

2. Leonard and Scott work together in an office. Scott wants to borrow some money from Leonard. Leonard doesn't want to lend the money. What is the conversation?

FRIDAY NIGHT RITUAL

INTERROGATING; PLEADING

QUESTION-WORD REVIEW

Characters: Mr. Wyman
Mrs. Wyman
Andy, age fourteen
Amy, age ten
Eugene, Andy's friend

Scene: Friday evening in the Wyman house. Mr. Wyman is in the living room. He is watching television. Amy is lying on the floor. She is also watching television. Mrs. Wyman is in the den. She is reading a book. A car horn sounds outside. Andy runs down the stairs and heads for the door.

Andy: Bye, everyone. I'm late.

Mr. Wyman: Just a minute, young man. Where are you going?

Andy: To a party. (*He comes into the living room.*)

Mr. Wyman: What party?

Andy: A birthday party for Gloria.

Mr. Wyman: Where is the party?

Andy: At Jane's.

Amy: She's silly.

Andy: Who's speaking to you?

Mr. Wyman: Who is Jane?

Andy: Dad, you know Jane.

Amy: She's the one with the crazy red hair.

(*Andy kicks Amy's foot.*)

Andy: Mother!

41

Mr. Wyman:	And with whom are you going?
Amy:	Yeah. Who are you going with?
Andy:	Everyone. Kay, John, Eugene—everyone. They're waiting now. (*He heads for the door.*)
Mr. Wyman:	Just a minute. How are you going?
Andy:	In Eugene's car.
Amy:	Whose car? Eugene has a motorbike.
Andy:	He has his father's car. Come on, Dad. They're waiting out front.
Mr. Wyman:	And who is Eugene? How old is he?
Andy:	You know Eugene. (*A car horn blows.*) There he is now. Please, Dad. I'm late.
Mr. Wyman:	When does the party end?
Andy:	At eleven. (*He puts on his jacket and heads for the door.*)
Mr. Wyman:	That's too late. You be back here by ten.
Andy:	Mother!
Mrs. Wyman:	What is it, dear? (*She comes in from the den with a book in her hand.*)
	(*A car horn blows.*)
Mr. Wyman:	Why is that boy blowing his horn?
Andy:	Because I'm late.
Mrs. Wyman:	It's all right. I know about the party.
Mr. Wyman:	All right, but you be home by ten.
Andy:	OK, OK. Ten o'clock. Bye. (*He rushes out the door.*)
	(*in the car*)
Eugene:	Hey! Why are you so late?
Andy:	Every Friday night my father asks the same questions: who, what, where, when, why, how! It never stops.
Eugene:	Forget it. (*He starts the car.*) By the way, who's coming to the party?
Andy:	Oh, no. You, too!!

A. Answer these questions. Remember, when possible use both short and long answers.

1. What is Mr. Wyman doing?   → Watching television. He's watching television.

2. What is Amy doing? → Watching television. She's also watching television.

3. Where is Andy going? → To a party. He's going to a party.

4. Where is the party? → At Jane's. The party is at Jane's.

5. Who is Andy going to the party with? → Everyone. He's going to the party with everyone.

6. How are they going to the party? → In Eugene's father's car. They're going to the party in Eugene's father's car.

7. When does the party end? → At eleven. The party ends at eleven.

8. What time does Andy have to be home? → By ten. He has to be home by ten.

9. Why is Eugene honking his horn? → Because Andy is late. Eugene is honking his horn because Andy is late.

10. What does Mr. Wyman do every Friday night? → Ask the same questions. He asks the same questions.

B. Improvise

1. You want to go on a weekend camping trip with friends from school. Your parents are worried about the idea. What is the conversation between you and your parents when you tell them about the trip?

2. You are a married woman. You plan to go out with your friends for the evening. Your husband is angry because he doesn't want you to go out alone. You are angry about his questions. What is the conversation?

THE DENTIST

EXPRESSING AGREEMENT OR DISAGREEMENT; CHANGING SOMEONE'S MIND
TOO, EITHER, AND *NEITHER*

Characters: Mrs. Price
Joseph, age six
Angela, age seven

Scene: The Price family's living room

Joseph: But I don't want to go to the dentist! I don't LIKE to go to the dentist!

Mrs. Price: I don't like to go to the dentist, either, but we have to.

Angela: I don't have to go. I don't have any cavities. (*She looks in the mirror with her mouth wide open.*)

Joseph: Neither do I. (*He opens his mouth wide.*)

Mrs. Price: Joe, you have to go to the dentist. It's time for a checkup.

Joseph: If I have to go, then Angela has to go, too.

Angela: I don't want to go!

Joseph: Neither do I.

Mrs. Price: We're going to the movies, too.

Angela: What?

Mrs. Price: We're going to the dentist and we're going to the movies, too. (*She starts to comb Joseph's hair.*)

Angela: I like the movies.

Joseph: I do, too.

Angela: But I don't like the dentist. (*She takes an apple from the table and bites into it.*)

Joseph: Neither do I. I don't like the dentist, either. (*He reaches for an apple.*)

45

(*Mrs. Price takes an apple and hands it to Joseph.*)

Mrs. Price: I don't like the dentist, EITHER, but it's necessary every six months.

Angela: I don't like the smell of the dentist's office.

Joseph: Neither do I.

Mrs. Price: Angela and Joseph, we're going to the dentist. Now find your coats and boots. It's raining.

(*They leave the room and return immediately.*)

Angela: I can't find my coat and I can't find my boots, either.

Joseph: Neither can I.

(*The phone rings.*)

Mrs. Price: Hello. Hello, Frank. I don't know. Angela doesn't want to go to the dentist and Joseph doesn't, either. I'll see . . . Joseph?

(*She gives the phone to Joseph.*)

Joseph: Hmm. Hmm. Yes, yes. Promise? Right after the dentist? . . . Daddy wants to talk to you, too.

(*He gives the phone to Angela. He leaves the room and returns immediately with his coat and Angela's.*)

Angela: A surprise? Me too? OK. (*She hangs up and starts to put on her coat.*) It's time to go to the dentist. I'm ready.

Joseph: I'm ready, too. (*He puts on his coat.*)

Mrs. Price: What? Angela wants to go to the dentist and Joseph does, too! How did he do it?

A. Answer the following questions. Use both short and long answers.

1. Does Joseph want to go to the dentist?

→ No, he doesn't. He doesn't want to go to the dentist.

2. Does Angela want to go to the dentist?

→ No, she doesn't. She doesn't want to go to the dentist, either.

3. Does Angela have any cavities?

→ She says she doesn't. She says she doesn't have any cavities.

4. Does Joseph have any cavities?

→ He thinks he doesn't. He thinks he doesn't have any cavities, either.

5. Where are they going after the dentist's?

→ To the movies. They're going to the movies after the dentist's.

6. Can Angela find her coat and boots? → No, she can't. She can't find her coat and boots.

7. Can Joseph find his coat and boots? → No, he can't. He can't find his coat and boots, either.

8. Who calls on the telephone? → The children's father. The children's father calls on the telephone.

9. Does he persuade the children to go to the dentist? → Yes, he does. He persuades the children to go to the dentist.

10. Is Mrs. Price surprised? → Yes, she is. Mrs. Price is surprised.

B. Improvise

1. Angela and Joseph are playing in the park with their six-year-old cousin, Thomas. They have difficulty agreeing on what to do. What is the conversation?

2. On a Saturday night, you and three friends are sitting in your living room. You are making plans for the evening, but you can't make up your minds. Every time someone suggests an activity, two disagree. What is the conversation?

MY GRASS IS GREENER

BOASTING; EXPRESSING COMPARISONS

COMPARATIVES IN *-ER*; SUPERLATIVES IN *-EST*

Characters: Alfred Quinn
Dennis Miller
Eddie Miller } all age nine or ten
Steve Lockwood
Jay Lockwood
Mrs. Miller
Mrs. Lockwood

Scene: A playground in a small town

Alfred: I'm higher than you. Whee . . . ! (*He swings up.*)

Dennis: No, you're not. I'm higher than you. (*He swings higher.*)

Alfred: No, you're not.

Dennis: I'm higher than you now. (*He swings up.*)

Eddie: I'm the highest. I'm the highest of all. (*He swings up and then points to a baseball bat on the ground.*) See my new bat?

Alfred: Yeah.

Dennis: It's BIG.

Eddie: Yes, it's bigger than yours.

Dennis: Hmm. I bet it isn't as GOOD as mine. (*He swings up.*)

Eddie: It's heavier than yours.

Alfred: My brother is a good baseball player. (*He jumps off the swing.*)

Eddie: Mine is, too. And he's better than your brother. (*He jumps off the swing, picks up his bat and starts to swing.*)

Steve: Hey, Alfred, Dennis, Eddie. Hi!

Jay: Guess what? (*He and his brother start playing catch.*)

Alfred: What?

Jay: We have a new TV.

Eddie: So what?

Steve: It's color!

Dennis: How big is it? (*He jumps off the swing.*)

Jay: Seventeen inches.

Alfred: Our TV is bigger than that.

(*Jay begins to kick the dust with his sneaker.*)

Steve: Our car is bigger than yours. (*He hits his baseball into his glove.*)

Jay: And our house is bigger than your house.

Alfred: But our house is NEWER than your house. And our grass is greener.

Steve: My father is bigger than your father.

Alfred: He is not.

Jay: Yes, he is. He's taller than your father.

Alfred: Well, he's fatter than my father.

Steve: My father is NOT fat. (*He stops throwing the ball.*)

Eddie: He is, too.

Jay: You better watch out! My brother is bigger than your brother. (*He throws his ball into his glove.*)

Eddie: My sister is smarter than yours. (*He swings around and falls.*)

Steve: She isn't!

Eddie: She is. She's the smartest student in the sixth grade.

Jay: My sister is the smartest student in the fifth grade.

Dennis: (*to Alfred*) Is his sister smarter than my sister?

Alfred: Gee, I don't know.

Dennis: My sister is smart.

Jay: But she isn't as smart as my sister!

Dennis: Your sister is dumb.

Steve: She is not!

Dennis: She is, too.

Jay:	She is not!
Dennis:	She is, too. She's the dumbest girl in the class.
Jay and Steve:	WHAT!?!
	(*Mrs. Miller and Mrs. Lockwood drive by.*)
Mrs. Miller:	There are the children in the playground.
Mrs. Lockwood:	Isn't it nice? They're such good friends.

A. Answer these questions. Remember, when possible use both short and long answers.

1. Where are the boys?
   → At the playground. The boys are at the playground.

2. On the swings, which boy is the highest?
   → Eddie. Eddie is the highest.

3. Is Eddie's baseball bat bigger than Dennis's?
   → Yes, it is. Eddie's baseball bat is bigger than Dennis's.

4. Whose TV is bigger than Jay and Steve's?
   → Alfred's. Alfred's TV is bigger than Jay and Steve's.

5. Whose car is bigger than Alfred's?
   → Jay and Steve's. Jay and Steve's car is bigger than Alfred's.

6. Whose house is bigger than Alfred's?
   → Jay and Steve's. Jay and Steve's house is bigger than Alfred's.

7. Whose house is newer than Jay and Steve's?
   → Alfred's. Alfred's house is newer than Jay and Steve's.

8. Whose father is taller than Alfred's father?
   → Jay and Steve's. Jay and Steve's father is taller than Alfred's father.

9. Whose sister is the smartest student in the sixth grade?
   → Eddie and Dennis's. Eddie and Dennis's sister is the smartest student in the sixth grade.

10. Whose sister is the smartest student in the fifth grade?
    → Jay and Steve's. Jay and Steve's sister is the smartest student in the fifth grade.

B. Improvise

1. What is the rest of Mrs. Miller and Mrs. Lockwood's conversation?

2. Sally Miller and Gladys Lockwood (the boys' sisters) are making cookies in the Lockwood kitchen. What is the conversation?

HOMESICK

HAVING AN ARGUMENT; COMPARING
COMPARATIVES AND SUPERLATIVES

Characters: Aaron Ramirez, an engineer born in Colombia, working in New York City
Diana Ramirez, born in Boston; married to Aaron
Ricardo Gomez, an engineer from Colombia, relocating to New York
Francine Gomez, a law student from Colombia; married to Ricardo

Scene: The Ramirezes' apartment in New York City. They and their guests, the Gomezes, are just sitting down to dinner.

Aaron: Welcome to the most wonderful city in the world!

Diana: And welcome to the most expensive city in the world. (*She glances at Aaron, then sighs.*)

(*Ricardo and Francine look at each other, then at Aaron and Diana, and then back to each other.*)

Aaron: (*He serves himself some chicken and then passes the dish.*) No, dear. Boston is more expensive than New York. New York is cheaper than Boston, and it's friendlier.

Diana: New York is friendlier than Boston? (*She turns to the Gomezes.*) He's joking, of course. Boston is friendlier. It's also smaller, quieter, and more comfortable. (*She serves some food and then looks at Aaron.*) It's quieter than New York. It's more comfortable than New York.

(*silence*)

Ricardo: (*He coughs.*) New York is more expensive than I expected.

Aaron: Oh, but it's more challenging. It's more exciting!

Diana: Yes, indeed. New York is certainly exciting. New York is the most exciting city in the world. Aaron LOVES it.

(*There is a loud thump from upstairs.*)

Ricardo: What's that?

Aaron: That's our upstairs neighbor. He practices Yoga a lot.

Diana: But he usually practices it at five o'clock in the morning. (*There is another loud thump. She smiles sarcastically.*) We have very interesting neighbors.

Aaron: The people here are more interesting than they are in BOSTON.

(*silence*)

Francine: We're looking for a one-bedroom apartment.

Ricardo: But it's difficult to find one that's not expensive.

Diana: Oh, yes. It's more difficult than you think.

Aaron: We're very lucky. This is a good apartment, and it's not very expensive.

Francine: Oh, it's a beautiful apartment! But what's that? (*She points to a gate across the window.*)

Diana: That's a security gate. New York is more dangerous than other cities.

Aaron: But, Diana, it's not the most dangerous city. (*He turns to the others.*) This building is safe. It's safer here than in any other part of the city.

Ricardo: We're looking for an apartment that's . . .

(*Drums and cymbals bang.*)

Francine: What's that?

Aaron: Our next-door neighbor. Drums. He's a musician. (*The drums get louder.*) There are more talented people in this building than . . .

Diana: And this neighbor is the most talented of them all. Why, he plays all the time . . . sometimes until three o'clock in the morning!

(*There is another loud thump from upstairs. The drums get louder. From now on, everyone speaks loudly because of the noise.*)

Ricardo: Oh, really? How interesting.

(*There are loud noises from below.*)

Francine: What's that?

Diana: We're over the boiler.

(*There is silence among the speakers. The drums get louder. The boiler makes more noises. There are more thumps from upstairs.*)

Ricardo: We want an apartment . . . (*Aaron stands up.*)

Aaron: (*shouting*) You want an apartment? OK, take this one. Diana, call your mother in Boston. Tell her we're coming for a long visit!

Diana: What? And leave the most wonderful city in the world?

A. Answer the following questions. Use both short and long answers.

1. Who likes Boston? → Diana. Diana likes Boston.

2. What are the Gomezes looking for? → An apartment. The Gomezes are looking for an apartment.

3. Are New York apartments cheap? → No, they're not. They're not cheap. They're expensive.

4. What does the upstairs neighbor do? → Practice Yoga. The upstairs neighbor practices Yoga.

5. When does he usually practice Yoga? → At five o'clock in the morning. He usually practices Yoga at five o'clock in the morning.

6. What does the next-door neighbor play? → The drums. The next-door neighbor plays the drums.

7. What do the Ramirezes live above? → The boiler. They live above the boiler.

8. Where does Diana's mother live? → Boston. Diana's mother lives in Boston.

9. Are Diana and Aaron happy tonight? → No, they're not. Diana and Aaron are not happy tonight. They're angry.

10. Who wants to leave New York City? → Aaron. Aaron wants to leave New York City.

B. Improvise

1. The building superintendent comes to fix a leak. Aaron complains to him about the noisy neighbors. What is the conversation?

2. What do Ricardo and Francine say to each other when they get back to their hotel?

IN THE PARK

EXPRESSING ABILITY OR INABILITY

SIMPLE PRESENT CONTRASTED WITH PRESENT CONTINUOUS;
CAN AND *CAN'T*

Characters: Phil
Judy
Elliot
Miriam

Scene: It is a summer afternoon in the park. Phil and Judy and Elliot and Miriam are strolling along a path.

Phil: Come on. Let's rent bicycles.

Elliot: Yes, look. Everyone is riding a bicycle.

Judy: (*Phil, Elliot, and Miriam hurry toward a bicycle stand. Judy pulls back.*) I can't.

Phil: What do you mean, you can't?

Judy: I only see boys' bikes. I'm wearing a skirt. I can't ride a boy's bicycle with a skirt.

Phil: Oh, Judy, try. It's a beautiful day for a ride.

Judy: No, I can't. I know.

Phil: Sigh. . . .

Judy: Go ahead. I can wait for you there. (*She points to a row of benches.*)

Phil: No, you can't.

Judy: Yes, I can. It's a resting place.

Phil: No . . . You two go ahead. We can't ride today. Maybe next week.

Elliot: OK. Come on, Miriam. (*He starts toward the bicycles.*)

Miriam: Elliot . . . I can't.

57

Elliot:	What do you mean?
Miriam:	Elliot, I can't ride a bicycle.
Elliot:	Yes, you can. You're wearing slacks.
Miriam:	But I can't ride a bicycle.
Elliot:	Why not?
Miriam:	I don't know how.
Elliot:	What? You can't ride a bicycle? Of course you can.
Miriam:	I can't.
Elliot:	Everyone can ride a bicycle.
Miriam:	Well, I can't. (*angry pause*) But I can ride a horse! (*She points to the bridle path.*)
Elliot:	Well, I can't. (*He kicks pebbles along the ground.*)
Judy:	The lake. Let's rent a boat!
Miriam:	That's a good idea! We can row around the lake.
Phil:	No.
Elliot:	Why not?
Phil:	I can't swim.
Elliot:	(*groan*) I can. I can save you. Don't worry. (*He laughs.*) Besides, the water is only three feet deep. You can walk in it.
Phil:	Well, OK.
Elliot:	Let's go. Oh, oh. Wait. We can't.
Phil:	What do you mean, we can't?
Elliot:	It's too expensive. I can't afford it.
Phil:	Oh, come on. I can lend you the money.
Elliot:	OK. Just until tomorrow.
	(*They rush to the lake.*)
Judy:	Oh, no.
Miriam:	What?!
Phil:	We can't rent a boat.
Elliot:	What's wrong NOW?!
Judy:	It's too late. Look. They're closing the gate!

A. Answer these questions. Remember, when possible use both short and long answers.

1. Why can't Judy ride a boy's bicycle? → She's wearing a skirt. Judy can't ride a boy's bicycle because she's wearing a skirt.

2. Why can't Miriam ride a bicycle? → She doesn't know how (to). Miriam can't ride a bicycle because she doesn't know how (to).

3. Who can ride a horse? → Miriam. Miriam can ride a horse.

4. Can Elliot ride a horse? → No, he can't. He can't ride a horse.

5. Can Phil swim? → No, he can't. He can't swim.

6. Why can he walk in the water? → It's only three feet deep. He can walk in the water because it's only three feet deep.

7. Why can't Elliot rent a boat? → He can't afford it. Elliot can't rent a boat because he can't afford it.

8. Can Phil lend Elliot the money? → Yes, he can. Phil can lend Elliot the money.

9. Why can't the couples rent a boat? → It's too late. The couples can't rent a boat because it's too late.

10. Can the couples make up their minds easily? → No, they can't. They can't make up their minds easily.

B. Improvise

1. Phil, Miriam, Elliot, and Judy are eating supper. They argue about their favorite soccer teams and players. What is the conversation?

2. On the way home, Phil gets angry with life in the city and begins to list all the things you cannot do in the city. The others remind him of what they did in the park that day and name other activities you can do in the city. What is the conversation?

CONSPIRATORS

CONSPIRING; TEASING

SOME AND *ANY*

Characters: Mr. King
Mrs. King
Bob, their son
Carol, Bob's wife

Scene: The King kitchen just before supper

Mr. King: Have some candy, Carol.

Bob: Carol's on a diet, Father. She can't have any sweets. (*He eats several pieces of candy.*)

Mrs. King: Your father is on a diet, too. He can't eat any candy.

(*Carol slips her father-in-law some candy. She sneaks some for herself.*)

Bob: Do you have any soda?

Mrs. King: Why, yes. There's some in the refrigerator.

Carol: I'll have some soda.

(*Mrs. King pours some soda into a glass.*)

Bob: No, Carol, you can't have any soda. (*He drinks some soda and then leaves the room.*)

Carol: You're right, dear. I can't have any soda.

(*Mr. King pours himself some soda, sips it, and gives it to Carol while Mrs. King is looking in the refrigerator.*)

Bob: (*He returns from the living room.*) Carol, are you eating candy? It's all gone.

Mr. King: I put it out of temptation. (*He stands in front of his daughter-in-law.*)

Carol: No, dear. I'm not eating any candy. (*She swallows some candy quickly.*)

Bob: Carol's on a diet. She can't have any sweets. (*He opens the refrigerator.*) I don't understand it, though. She's not losing any weight.

Mrs. King: Your father isn't losing any weight, either.

Bob: Mom, do you have any pie?

Mrs. King: For dessert. First, I have some steak, some homemade bread, some sweet corn, some potatoes, and salad. Sit down.

(*They all go into the dining room for dinner.*)

Mr. King: You're not any help, Margaret.

Bob: Remember, Carol can't have any potatoes or any bread.

(*Carol and Mr. King look at their salad and steak and look very sad.*)

Mr. King: Have some bread, Carol. I can't have any. (*He passes the bread plate.*)

Bob: Carol can't have any bread, Father. (*He takes the plate.*)

Mr. King: (*He gets up, walks into the kitchen, and returns.*) Try some corn, Carol.

Carol: I can't have any corn. (*She eats her salad.*)

Mrs. King: (*to Mr. King*) Remember, dear. You can have some corn but just a little.

Bob: This bread is delicious. I'm sorry you can't have any, Carol.

Mr. King: Have some mashed potatoes, Carol.

Bob: She can't have any potatoes, Father. (*He reaches for another ear of corn.*)

Mr. King: I admire you, Carol. I don't have any will power.

Bob: She needs some help. Some more steak, please, Mom.

Mr. King: Excuse me. I'll be right back. (*He gets up and goes into the kitchen.*)

Mrs. King: Save some appetite for the pie, Bob.

Mr. King: (*He calls from the kitchen.*) Phone call for you, Carol.

(*Carol goes into the kitchen. Mr. King puts his finger against his lips and points to the bread box by the phone. Carol opens it to find a plate with an ear of corn and some pie on it. She holds the phone as if she is speaking and begins to eat the pie.*)

A. Answer these questions. Remember, when possible use both short and long answers.

1. Who are Carol and Bob visiting? → His parents. They're visiting his parents.

62

2. Why can't Carol eat candy?   → She's on a diet. Carol can't eat candy because she's on a diet.

3. Who else is on a diet?   → Mr. King. Mr. King is also on a diet.

4. Can Carol have any soda?   → No, she can't. She can't have any soda.

5. Does Mrs. King help Carol with her diet?   → No, she doesn't. She doesn't help Carol with her diet.

6. Can Carol have any bread?   → No, she can't. She can't have any bread.

7. Does Mr. King keep to his diet?   → No, he doesn't. He doesn't keep to his diet.

8. What does Mrs. King prepare for dinner?   → Steak, potatoes, corn, bread, salad, and pie. Mrs. King prepares steak, potatoes, corn, bread, salad, and pie.

9. Is there really a phone call for Carol?   → No, there isn't. There isn't a phone call for Carol.

10. What is in the bread box in the kitchen?   → An ear of corn and some pie. There's an ear of corn and some pie in the bread box.

B. Improvise

1. Later, Mrs. King finds Mr. King eating cake and begins to scold him. He gets angry with her for having cake and other fattening foods in the house. What is the conversation?

2. Harold and Elaine are a married couple. They have just moved into a new apartment. Harold wants to buy a lot of furniture and new kitchen equipment. Elaine thinks they can't afford these things. They argue. What is the conversation?

JOGGING?

NEGOTIATING A COMPROMISE
INFINITIVES AND GERUNDS

Characters: Brenda, a twenty-nine-year-old lawyer
Eric, a twenty-nine-year-old engineer
Gail, a thirty-year-old writer
Ted, a thirty-year-old tax accountant

Scene: The four friends are sitting in Ted's living room after brunch on a Sunday afternoon. They all live in the same apartment building.

Brenda: Let's go for a walk.

Eric: Oh, not now. I want to relax. I'd like to sit around and watch television.

Ted: It's a beautiful day. Let's go jogging. I love to jog.

Brenda: I do, too. And I need to exercise.

Eric: Boy, you stopped smoking and now you're a health addict. I just want to relax and watch the football game.

Gail: You always want to relax.

Eric: I work hard all week. I enjoy doing nothing on the weekends.

Ted: He enjoys doing nothing on the weekends. (*He sighs.*) Jogging is good for you. It will make you feel better.

Eric: I feel fine. I plan to sit here and do nothing.

Brenda: Well, I have to do some work. If we aren't going to jog, I'll do my report for tomorrow.

Gail: I'd like to go to the movies.

Ted: Let's jog and then we can go to the movies.

Eric: I stopped jogging a year ago. You three go. I want to watch television.

Ted: But you didn't go jogging regularly. That's why you didn't like to run. You're out of shape.

Eric: I enjoyed jogging! But not now. You three go ahead.

Brenda: No. If we can't go jogging together, let's stay here. I know. Let's play music.

Eric: Music!

Ted: Music. That's a good idea. I'll get my violin.

Eric: Violin?

Gail: I play the clarinet! You get your violin, and I'll get my clarinet.

Eric: Clarinet?

Brenda: I'm trying to learn the guitar. I'll go get it.

Eric: Guitar?

Ted: Yeah! We can practice playing together.

Eric: I thought you wanted to jog. You want to jog? Let's go jogging.

A. Answer these questions. Remember, when possible use both short and long answers.

1. What does Brenda do? → She's a lawyer.

2. What does Eric do? → He's an engineer.

3. What does Gail do? → She's a writer.

4. What does Ted do? → He's a tax accountant.

5. Where are the four friends? → In Ted's living room. They're in Ted's living room.

6. What does Brenda want to do? → Go for a walk. Brenda wants to go for a walk.

7. What does Eric want to do? → Watch television. Eric wants to watch television.

8. What does Ted want to do? → Go jogging. Ted wants to go jogging.

9. What does Brenda finally suggest? → That they play music. Brenda suggests that they play music.

10. What does Eric finally suggest? → That they go jogging. Eric finally suggests that they go jogging.

B. Improvise

1. What is the conversation when the four return from jogging?

2. Mieko, Jorge, Chris, and Rudy are foreign students in New York City. They study English together. One night after class they try to make plans to do something Friday night. What is the conversation?

A TASTE OF NEW YORK

ORDERING FOOD
SIMPLE PRESENT; COUNTABLES AND UNCOUNTABLES

Characters: A waiter
Jean-Pierre
Jules } tourists from France
Claudine
François

Scene: A New York restaurant. This is Claudine's second trip to the United States. It is the first trip for the others. They are studying the menu when the waiter comes up.

Waiter: May I help you?

Jean-Pierre: Please. But first, what's . . . "ravioli"? (*He reads from the menu.*)

Waiter: (*He speaks quickly.*) Pasta with beef and tomato sauce.

Jean-Pierre: Pardon me?

Waiter: Ravioli is pasta with beef and tomato sauce.

Jules: What's the "chef's salad" . . . "sal . . . ad" . . . (*He stumbles over the words.*)

Waiter: (*His tone is curt and rude.*) A salad.

Claudine: But what's in it?

Waiter: Lettuce, tomatoes, carrots, green beans, onions, cheese, and ham. May I have your order?

François: What's the "chef's special" today?

Waiter: Today's special is a hamburger, french-fried potatoes, and a salad. Now, please, may I have your order?

François: (*He turns to Claudine.*) What's a hamburger?

Claudine: A hamburger is ground beef on a roll.

69

François: I want the chef's special.

Waiter: (*He speaks quickly.*) Medium, medium-rare, rare, or well done?

François: Pardon me?

Waiter: How do you want your hamburger?

François: On a roll.

Waiter: Yes, but how do you want it cooked—medium, medium-rare, rare, or well done?

François: What does he mean? (*Claudine translates medium, medium-rare, rare, and well done. The waiter taps his pencil on his pad.*) Oh. (*He speaks to Claudine again. Then he speaks to the waiter.*) Rare.

Waiter: Fine. Next?

Claudine: The chef's salad, please.

Waiter: (*He writes down the orders.*) And you?

Jean-Pierre: I want ravioli.

Jules: I want the chef's salad.

Waiter: Do you want anything to drink?

Jules: Coffee. Claudine, what do you want?

Claudine: Coffee.

Jules: Jean-Pierre?

Jean-Pierre: Coffee.

(*François speaks to Claudine.*)

Claudine: My friend wants tea with lemon.

Jules: We want three coffees and one tea.

Claudine: With lemon.

Jean-Pierre: Do you have "café au lait"?

Waiter: What's that?

Claudine: It's French coffee with hot milk.

Waiter: We only serve American coffee here.

Jean-Pierre: Never mind. Bring three coffees and one tea.

(*The waiter leaves.*)

Claudine:	The waiter is rude. Shall we leave a tip?
Jules:	What's a tip?
Claudine:	Money for the waiter. Besides the bill.
Jules:	Oh, yes. Of course.
Jean-Pierre:	Is it necessary?
Claudine:	It's not necessary, but it's a custom to give extra money for good service.
François:	Maybe we should have tipped in advance!

A. Answer these questions. Remember, when possible use both short and long answers.

1. Where are the tourists? → In a New York restaurant. They're in a New York restaurant.

2. How much English do they know? → A little. They know a little English.

3. How does the waiter speak? → Quickly. He speaks quickly.

4. Is the waiter a good waiter? → No, he isn't. He's a rude waiter.

5. How does François want his hamburger cooked? → Rare. He wants his hamburger rare.

6. What does Claudine order? → The chef's salad. She orders the chef's salad.

7. What Jean-Pierre want? → Ravioli. He wants ravioli.

8. What does Jules want? → The chef's salad. He wants the chef's salad.

9. Does the restaurant serve "café au lait"? → No, it doesn't. It only serves American coffee.

10. Does the waiter deserve a tip? → No, he doesn't. He doesn't deserve a tip.

B. Improvise

1. When the waiter brings the order, he serves the wrong food. Claudine gets the ravioli. Jean-Pierre gets the chef's salad. François's hamburger is well done. What is the conversation?

2. At a fast-food restaurant where customers sit at a counter, Roz and Gay are ordering hamburgers and coffee. The waitress is pleasant but confused. The restaurant is crowded; Gary and Don are standing behind Roz and Gay waiting to take their seats. Everyone is hurried and impatient. What is the conversation?

A PICNIC

FLAUNTING

COUNTABLES AND UNCOUNTABLES

Characters: Bert Wright
Sarah Wright
Ronny, their son
Molly Fontaine
Norman Fontaine
Matthew, their son

Scene: A camping site in the country. On Memorial Day weekend, Bert and Sarah are preparing a picnic dinner outside their tent. The Fontaines come out of their tent. Earlier that day, the two couples had agreed to eat dinner together.

Bert: What's for dinner?

Sarah: Franks and beans. (*She starts unpacking some food from a container.*)

Molly: We have lobster. And potato salad.

Sarah: Lobster? (*She walks over to look in a bag with live lobsters in it.*)

Ronny: We never have lobster. (*He peeks into the bag.*)

Sarah: Let's see. Mustard, relish, ketchup, potato chips.

Norman: Lettuce, tomatoes, avocado, cucumbers. (*He starts to cut up the fresh vegetables.*)

Sarah: Our salad is all ready. (*She puts it out on the picnic table.*)

Norman: Wait. Wait. I have a tablecloth. (*He spreads out a tablecloth.*)

Ronny: Here are the knives and forks. (*He brings out plastic knives and forks.*)

Matthew: HERE are the knives and forks. (*He brings out silverware.*)

(*Sarah and Bert look at each other.*)

Bert: (*whispering*) Where are the candlesticks? (*pause*) Let's have some music. (*He turns on a transistor radio and gets loud pop music.*)

Molly: Let's CHOOSE our music. (*She brings out a tape recorder and puts in a cassette of classical music.*) I have jazz, too. For later.

Norman: (*humming to himself*) Tea with lemon.

Sarah: What? (*She opens a jar of instant tea.*)

Norman: I'm getting tea ready for after dinner. How's the fire going?

Molly: Fine! The water is almost ready for the lobster. (*She is perspiring and wipes her forehead.*)

Bert: Nothing like hot dogs cooked over an open fire. (*Bert fixes sticks to use to roast the hot dogs.*)

Matthew: Can I have a hot dog?

Ronny: Dad, can I have a lobster?

(*Bert and Sarah shake their heads.*)

Bert: The lobster isn't ready yet.

Sarah: What are you doing now?

Norman: Opening up the wine. (*Norman is struggling with a cork screw.*)

Bert: We have beer.

Molly: We must have wine with lobster.

Norman: (*The cork breaks.*) Ooh.

Molly: There it goes! (*She drops the lobsters into the water.*) It takes about twenty minutes.

Bert: Here we are. (*Bert begins to serve the hot dogs.*)

Matthew: Hmm. Can I have a hot dog?

Molly: Let me taste it. Mmm. Just one, while I'm waiting.

Norman: Give me a bite. Mmm. Sarah, pass the potato chips.

(*Norman, Molly, and Matthew eat the hot dogs that Bert put on the table.*)

Molly: Say, Bert, will you watch the lobster? (*She reaches for another hot dog.*)

(*Norman opens a can of beer.*)

A. Answer the following questions. Use short and long answers when possible.

1. What do Bert and Sarah have for dinner? → Franks and beans. Bert and Sarah have franks and beans for dinner.

2. What do Norman and Molly have for dinner? → Lobster. Norman and Molly have lobster for dinner.

3. What is Sarah's reaction when she hears about the lobster? → She's surprised. Sarah is surprised when she hears about the lobster.

4. What does Sarah have in jars? → Mustard, relish, and ketchup. Sarah has mustard, relish, and ketchup in jars.

5. What does Norman have for his fresh salad? → Lettuce, tomatoes, avocado, and cucumbers. Norman has lettuce, tomatoes, avocado, and cucumbers for his salad.

6. What kind of knives and forks does Ronny put out on the table? → Plastic. Ronny puts plastic knives and forks on the table.

7. What kind of music does Molly want to play? → Classical music. Molly wants to play classical music.

8. Which family is more informal? → The Wrights. The Wrights are more informal than the Fontaines.

9. Which family has the easier meal to prepare? → The Wrights. The Wrights have the easier meal to prepare.

10. Whose food is more tempting? → The Wrights'. The Wrights' food is more tempting.

B. Improvise

1. Daryl and Gus are in a small grocery store ordering food for the week. The prices are high, but they don't have time to go to another store. What is the conversation between them and the grocer?

2. Dean has brought his fiancée, Patricia, home for dinner. His father approves of the marriage. His mother doesn't. She really doesn't ever want Dean to marry. What is the conversation?

RUSH-HOUR DELAY

EXPRESSING NEED AND OFFERING HELP
HOW MANY; NEED AND WANT

Characters: A subway clerk
Vic Martinelli, a tourist from Italy
First man
Second man
First woman
Second woman } in line behind Vic
Third man
Third woman

Scene: A busy subway change booth. It is rush hour.

Clerk: How many?

Vic: What?

Clerk: How many tokens do you want?

Vic: How many do I need?

Clerk: What?!

Vic: How many tokens do I need to get to Fourth Street?

Clerk: One.

Vic: One, please. . . And how many tokens do I need to get back?

Clerk: You need one to get there and one to get back. You need two, but you can have as many as you want. How many do you want?

Vic: Two, please. (*He hands the clerk a twenty-dollar bill.*)

Clerk: (*He sighs.*) I can't change a twenty-dollar bill.

Vic: That's all I have. (*He looks through his pocket for change.*)

Clerk: Sorry. Next!

Vic:	I don't have anything else.
	(*The people in line begin to get impatient.*)
Clerk:	Look, mister, there are a lot of people behind you. I can't change a twenty-dollar bill. Move along.
Vic:	What? (*He stands there confused.*)
Clerk:	Move along.
Vic:	But. . .
First Man:	What's the problem? (*He steps up to the window.*)
Clerk:	I can't change a twenty-dollar bill. He wants two tokens and only has a twenty-dollar bill. I can't take it. How many do YOU want?
Second Man:	Wait a minute. Why can't you take his twenty-dollar bill? (*He steps up to the window.*)
Clerk:	I don't have enough CHANGE. Besides, read the sign. (*He points to a sign which reads: "Clerks are not required to accept bills larger than ten dollars."*)
First Man:	You don't need to yell!
Clerk:	Who's YELLING?!!
First Woman:	Can't you see he's a visitor? Be helpful.
Clerk:	But I don't have any change!
First Woman:	Well, it's a shame! The man doesn't know the city, and look what happens at his first token booth. The clerk yells at him. How many visitors do you yell at?
Clerk:	I'M NOT YELLING!!
First Woman:	How many countries have YOU visited?
Clerk:	None.
First Woman:	How many languages do you know?
Clerk:	One.
Second Woman:	How many tokens do you want, young man?
Clerk:	He wants two tokens.
Vic:	I want two tokens.
Clerk:	He has a twenty-dollar bill, and I can't take a twenty-dollar bill.
Second Woman:	Just a minute. Maybe I can change your bill. (*She opens her purse.*)
First Man:	Right. Change his twenty-dollar bill.

(*Everyone searches for change.*)

Second Woman: Oh, dear. I have only three dollars.

First Man: Maybe I can change it.

Third Man: I want to catch the next train.

First Man: Can anyone change a twenty-dollar bill?

Third Man: No.

Second Man: I can't.

Third Woman: Neither can I.

(*Sighs and groans from the commuters until at last the clerk reaches into his own pocket and takes out his billfold.*)

Clerk: Here, . . . Here, . . . HERE. (*He gives Vic twenty one-dollar bills, takes one back, and pushes two tokens through the window.*) Now, please, mister, please move along! NEXT!

A. Answer these questions. Remember, when possible use both short and long answers.

1. Where is Vic?
   → In a subway station. He's in a subway station.

2. What is rush hour?
   → The time of day most people travel to and from work. It is the busiest time of day for traveling.

3. How many tokens does Vic need?
   → Two. He needs two tokens.

4. Are there many people behind Vic?
   → Yes, there are. There are many people behind Vic.

5. Why can't the clerk take Vic's twenty-dollar bill?
   → He doesn't have enough change. The sign says he is not required to accept bills larger than ten dollars.

6. Does the clerk yell?
   → Yes, he does. He yells.

7. How many foreign countries has the clerk visited?
   → None. The clerk hasn't visited any foreign countries.

8. How many languages does the clerk know?
   → One. He knows English.

9. How many people try to help Vic?
   → A lot of people. A lot of people try to help Vic.

79

10. Who changes Vic's money?   → The clerk. The clerk changes Vic's money.

B. Improvise

1. On Saturday afternoon, Luke and Walter are arguing. Walter wants to go to the movies, but Luke wants to go shopping to buy books for school. Luke thinks Walter is irresponsible. Walter thinks Luke studies too much. What is the conversation?

2. Mira and Stan are two Americans visiting Yugoslavia. They are lost and tired. They are looking for a hotel along the Adriatic coast but cannot find one. They stop to ask directions from two shopkeepers. Only one of the shopkeepers speaks English. What is the conversation?

PATIENCE

ORDERING GROCERIES

SIMPLE PRESENT WITH *HOW MUCH* AND *HOW MANY*

Characters: Mr. Pallas, a storeowner
Jennifer, a customer
Mrs. Nevins, an old woman
A delivery man
Carl, a customer
Mac, Mr. Pallas's assistant
Another customer

Scene: A small grocery store. It is early in the morning in Mr. Pallas's grocery store. The delivery man delivers dairy products to the store every day. The customers are crowded in the small store.

Mr. Pallas:	Next?
Jennifer:	How much is a pound of tomatoes?
Mr. Pallas:	Ninety-nine cents.
Jennifer:	That's expensive. How many tomatoes are in a pound?
Mr. Pallas:	Usually three. Sometimes four if they're small.
Jennifer:	I want one pound, then.
	(*Mr. Pallas weighs three tomatoes on the scale.*)
Mrs. Nevins:	(*She enters the store.*) How much is your corned beef today?
Mr. Pallas:	Just a minute, lady. I have a customer.
	(*A delivery man enters the store. He's pushing a cart of dairy goods.*)
Delivery Man:	Excuse me. Excuse me. I'm coming through!
	(*Carl enters the store and picks up a loaf of bread. He has money in his hand.*)

Carl:	How much is a loaf of bread?
Mr. Pallas:	(*to Carl*) Be with you in a minute. (*to Jennifer*) Anything else?
Jennifer:	Three cans of chicken soup.
	(*Mrs. Nevins begins to feel the fruit and vegetables.*)
Mr. Pallas:	Lady, please don't touch the fruit. (*to Jennifer*) How many cans of soup?
Jennifer:	Three.
Delivery Man:	(*shouting from the back of the store*) How much butter do you want?
Mr. Pallas:	What?
Delivery Man:	How much butter do you want?
Mr. Pallas:	Twenty-five pounds.
Carl:	All I want is a loaf of bread. How much is a loaf of bread? (*He holds out the bread and some money.*)
Mr. Pallas:	(*Mrs. Nevins continues to feel the fruit.*) Madam, please don't touch the fruit.
Mac:	(*He shouts from the back of the store.*) Mr. Pallas, how much milk do you want?
Mr. Pallas:	What?
Mac:	(*He shouts a little louder from the back of the store.*) How many quarts of milk do you want?
Mr. Pallas:	Sixty, sixty . . . Wait . . . How many do we have now?
Mac:	About twenty.
Mr. Pallas:	Take forty, then. . . . Anything else, miss? (*He turns to Jennifer and puts three cans of soup on the counter.*)
Carl:	How much is a loaf of bread?
Mrs. Nevins:	Is your fruit fresh?
Mr. Pallas:	Yes, my fruit is fresh.
Jennifer:	A pound of cheese, two cans of tuna fish, a can of orange juice . . .
Mac:	(*He shouts from the back of the store.*) How many pints of cream?
Mr. Pallas:	What?
Mac:	(*He shouts a little louder from the back of the store.*) How many pints of cream?
Mr. Pallas:	(*He shouts to the delivery man.*) How much is it today?

Delivery Man:	(*He shouts from the back of the store.*) Seventy cents a pint.
Mr. Pallas:	That's too much.
Delivery Man:	I deliver the goods; I don't make the prices. How many pints do you want?
Carl:	Just a loaf of bread. . . . I want just ONE loaf of bread.
Mr. Pallas:	(*He shouts.*) Mac, take thirty pints of cream. (*to Jennifer*) How many cans of orange juice?
Jennifer:	Just one.
Mrs. Nevins:	How much are your oranges?
Carl:	A loaf of bread. . .
Mrs. Nevins:	How much are your oranges?
Mr. Pallas:	Two for sixty cents.
Carl:	Bread. . . . (*He squeezes the loaf of bread.*)
Jennifer:	A pound of ham, please. (*She reads from her list.*)
Mac:	How many eggs do we want?
Mr. Pallas:	Three crates.
Jennifer:	How many slices in a pound? (*She watches Mr. Pallas slice the ham.*)
Mr. Pallas:	Lady, please don't touch the fruit. (*He watches Mrs. Nevins as he slices.*)
Carl:	Just bread. All I want is a loaf of bread.
Mrs. Nevins:	How much is one orange?
Customer:	May I have a quart of milk?
Carl:	. . . Bread! . . .
Jennifer:	And a bottle of ginger ale and . . .
Delivery Man:	Sign here. (*He hands Mr. Pallas a receipt.*)
Mrs. Nevins:	This one looks good. (*She takes an orange from the bottom of the pile. The oranges fall all over the floor.*)
	(*Carl screams and leaves without his bread. Mr. Pallas hits his head on the counter. Jennifer covers her face as she laughs. The delivery man laughs.*)

A. Answer these questions. Remember, when possible use both short and long answers.

    1. Is Mr. Pallas's store peaceful
and quiet?   → No, it isn't. It's busy and confusing.

84

2. How much is a pound of tomatoes? → Ninety-nine cents. A pound of tomatoes is ninety-nine cents.

3. How many cans of soup does Jennifer want? → Three. She wants three cans of soup.

4. How much butter does Mr. Pallas want? → Twenty-five pounds. He wants twenty-five pounds of butter.

5. How many quarts of milk does Mr. Pallas want? → Forty. He wants forty quarts of milk.

6. How many pints of cream does Mr. Pallas want? → Thirty. He wants thirty pints of cream.

7. How many cans of orange juice does Jennifer want? → One. She wants one can of juice.

8. How many eggs does Mr. Pallas want? → Three crates. He wants three crates of eggs.

9. How much is a loaf of bread? → We don't know.

10. Is Carl very happy? → No, he isn't. He isn't very happy.

B. Improvise

1. After the oranges are picked up, after Jennifer and Carl leave, Mr. Pallas waits on Mrs. Nevins. What is the conversation?

2. Becky and Diane are returning to Los Angeles from a tour of Europe. They are coming through customs at the airport. The customs inspector reads their statements as he asks them what they have to declare. The customs inspector is suspicious. The two women are nervous. What is the conversation?

A FOREIGN LANGUAGE

MAKING EXCUSES; COMPLAINING

SIMPLE PAST: /t/ AND /d/ ENDINGS

Characters: Lucy
Heinrich
Hilda
Giorgio
André
Rafael

Scene: Students of English as a foreign language are waiting for class to begin. They are standing in the corridor outside the classroom.

Lucy: Did you do the homework?

Heinrich: No, I didn't. My in-laws came to dinner last night, and they stayed for hours. Did YOU do it?

Lucy: No. My house was too noisy. My brother and his friends played disco music all night. I asked them to be quiet, but it was impossible to study.

Hilda: I watched television.

Giorgio: Me too.

Hilda: Did you watch the basketball game? It was a good game.

Giorgio: No, I didn't. I watched "60 Minutes."

André: "60 Minutes"? Why did you watch that? You missed a good show on Channel 7. It was a special. It starred Frank Sinatra.

Giorgio: I always watch "60 Minutes."

Heinrich: Was it interesting?

Giorgio: Who knows? My sister was on the telephone in the same room, and she talked and talked. I couldn't HEAR anything, but it LOOKED good.

Hilda: I enjoyed the basketball game, but I missed the end.

Lucy:	Why?
Hilda:	A friend called. By the time I finished the conversation, the game was over.
Heinrich:	Here comes Rafael.
Lucy:	(*to Rafael*) Did you do the homework?
Rafael:	Well, yes and no.
Heinrich:	What does THAT mean?
Rafael:	I looked at the lesson, but I didn't understand it.
Giorgio:	What was the trouble?
Rafael:	We studied regular verb forms in class last week, but the homework used irregular verbs: sing-sang, take-took, eat-ate. What happened to all the -ed endings we learned?

A. Answer these questions. Remember, when possible use both short and long answers.

1. Did Heinrich do his homework? → No, he didn't. He didn't do his homework.

2. Why didn't Heinrich do his homework? → Because his in-laws came to dinner and stayed for hours. He didn't do his homework because his in-laws came to dinner and stayed for hours.

3. Did Lucy do her homework? → No, she didn't. She didn't do her homework.

4. Why didn't Lucy do her homework? → Because her house was too noisy. Lucy didn't do her homework because her house was too noisy.

5. Why didn't Hilda do her homework? → Because she watched television. Hilda didn't do her homework because she watched television.

6. Why didn't Giorgio do his homework? → Because he watched television. Giorgio didn't do his homework because he watched television.

7. Why did Hilda miss the end of the game? → Because a friend called. Hilda missed the end of the game because a friend called.

8. Who did the homework? → Rafael. Rafael did the homework.

9. Did Rafael understand the homework? → No, he didn't. Rafael didn't understand the homework.

10. Why didn't Rafael understand the homework?

→ Because the students studied regular verb forms in class, but the homework used irregular verbs. Rafael didn't understand the homework because the students studied regular verb forms in class, but the homework used irregular verbs.

B. Improvise

1. In class the students complain about the English language to the teacher. What is the conversation?

2. Louis, Roy, Liz, and Margaret are in the cafeteria. Louis was mugged the night before. The others ask him what happened. What is the conversation?

FROSTING

EXPLAINING; ASSUMING RESPONSIBILITY

IRREGULAR PAST

Characters: Mrs. Schulman
Mrs. Klein, Mrs. Schulman's sister
Robert Schulman, age twelve
Ann Schulman, age thirteen
Roger Klein, Mrs. Schulman's nephew, age eleven
Tim
Marvin
Jack   } Robert's friends
Tony
Nelson

Scene: It is Sunday afternoon. Mrs. Schulman walks into her kitchen with her sister. The kitchen is a mess; dirty dishes and pots and pans are everywhere. Robert, Ann, and Roger are trying to clean the room. They look very guilty.

Mrs. Schulman: What happened here? (*She looks at the mess.*)

Mrs. Klein: What did you do? (*She sniffs to see what is burning.*)

Robert: I made a cake.

Ann: He TRIED to make a cake. I came home and found him . . .

Roger: I saw everything. Robert and his friends . . . (*Ann glares at him. Robert gives him a push.*)

Mrs. Schulman: Where is MY cake? (*She looks under a newspaper and then under a dish towel.*)

Robert: We ate it. (*He picks a piece of paper up.*)

Mrs. Schulman: I left a message on the table. It said, "Do not touch this cake." (*She sits at the table with her hands on her head.*)

Roger:	I found it on the floor, but . . . (*Robert kicks him.*)
Robert:	It fell on the floor. We didn't see it till it was too late.
Mrs. Klein:	My son didn't eat any. (*She puts her hand on Roger's shoulder.*)
Ann:	Yes, he did. He took the first piece.
Mrs. Schulman:	You knew the church bazaar was tonight! The whole cake? (*She goes to the refrigerator and groans after she opens the door.*) Where is the case of soda?
Ann:	We drank it.
Mrs. Klein:	The three of you ate a whole cake and drank a whole case of soda?
Ann:	The baseball team was here.
Mrs. Klein:	You had the baseball team here?
Mrs. Schulman:	How could you? I told you . . .
Mrs. Klein:	Irresponsible teen-agers.
Robert:	I forgot. We were hungry, and when we saw the cake we ate it.
Roger:	Then we found the note on the floor.
Mrs. Schulman:	What did you do with the plate it was on?
Ann:	We threw it away. (*She points to the rubbish.*)
Roger:	Tim and Jack were fooling around and they hit the table and . . .
Robert:	It broke. It fell and broke.
Mrs. Schulman:	I left the house for an hour. Irresponsible teen-agers.
Mrs. Klein:	Irresponsible.
	(*The door then opens and Tim walks in with a package.*)
Tim:	Hey! I found a cake. Hi, Mrs. Schulman.
Marvin:	I found a store open and bought a cake.
Jack:	Here's a case of soda. (*He backs into the room carrying a case.*)
Tony:	Here's a case of soda. (*He holds the back door open with his foot as he comes in with a case.*)
Nelson:	I bought a cake, Mrs. Schulman.
	(*Mrs. Schulman, Robert, and Roger looked shocked. Ann sighs with relief. Mrs. Klein smiles in amazement.*)

A. Answer the questions. Use both short and long answers.

1. What did Mrs. Schulman find when she walked into the kitchen? → A mess. She found dirty dishes and pots and pans everywhere.

2. What did Robert try to do? → Make a cake. Robert tried to make a cake.

3. Why did Robert try to make a cake? → He and his friends ate his mother's cake.

4. What did Mrs. Schulman leave on the kitchen table? → A message. Mrs. Schulman left a message on the kitchen table.

5. What did the message say? → "Do not touch this cake." The message said, "Do not touch this cake."

6. Where did the boys find the message? → On the floor. The boys found the message on the floor.

7. When did the boys find the message? → After they ate the cake. The boys found the message after they ate the cake.

8. Did Roger eat any cake? → Yes, he did. He ate the first piece.

9. Who drank the case of soda? → The baseball team. The baseball team drank the case of soda.

10. Were the teen-agers irresponsible? → No, they weren't. They replaced the cake and soda.

B. Improvise

1. Roger and Robert meet the next day. What is their conversation?

2. Irene and Glen drive to the movies. Then Glen stands in line while Irene parks the car. The line is long and people are impatient. When Glen lets Irene in line, other people behind him become angry. What is the conversation?

SPRING FEVER

EXPRESSING LOVE AND DISAPPOINTMENT

REVIEW: SIMPLE PRESENT; SIMPLE PAST;
PRESENT CONTINUOUS; *WAS* AND *WERE*

Characters: Mrs. Wagner
Mrs. Fanelli
Ken Fanelli, age ten
Jane Fanelli, age twelve
Charlie Wagner, age twelve

Scene: The Fanellis and Wagners are next-door neighbors in a small town. It is Saturday on a spring morning. Mrs. Fanelli is painting house shutters. Mrs. Wagner is in her yard planting flowers. Ken, Jane, and Charlie are friends. Ken and Charlie usually play baseball together on Saturday.

Mrs. Wagner: What a beautiful day! The trees are budding. The grass is growing. The birds are singing. Listen. (*She rests from planting.*)

Mrs. Fanelli: Ah, spring! The kids are playing baseball. Look. (*She points to a broken window and holds up a baseball.*)

Mrs. Wagner: Kids. Last year they broke our window. But look at my bulbs. I planted them a month ago, and they're blooming.

Mrs. Fanelli: I planted some a month ago and the dogs dug them up. (*She picks up a dead bulb.*)

Mrs. Wagner: There are Ken and Jane. I wonder where Charlie is. They're usually together.

Mrs. Fanelli: Ken, where is Charlie?

Ken: I don't know. All he does is daydream. . . . He used to be a good baseball player. (*He slaps the ball into his baseball glove.*)

Jane: He's in the backyard, helping his father.

Ken: (*He looks hurt.*) How do you know?

95

Mrs. Wagner:	Here he is.
	(*Charlie walks around the corner of the house holding a hose. He sprays the lawn.*)
Charlie:	I'm watering the lawn. Hi, Jane . . . (*He looks at Jane and water from the hose hits Ken.*) Oops.
Jane:	Hi.
Ken:	Watch it. (*He backs away from Charlie.*)
Charlie:	Hey, I'm sorry.
Mrs. Wagner:	Charlie, you're daydreaming again.
Ken:	He's always daydreaming. (*He slaps the ball into his glove.*)
Charlie:	Mother, can I water here yet?
Mrs. Wagner:	Yes. I must get back to work. (*She picks up her garden tools.*)
Mrs. Fanelli:	Me too. (*She shakes her head as she picks up a paintbrush.*) I bought these shutters two years ago and they need paint already.
Mrs. Wagner:	I love planting. (*She returns to work.*)
Mrs. Fanelli:	I hate painting. (*She returns to work.*)
	(*Charlie walks toward the front walk, looks at Jane, and sprays Ken.*)
Ken:	Hey, watch it.
Jane:	Do you need help?
Ken:	Does he need help! You never help ME!
Charlie:	Maybe with the car. I'm going to wash the car after I water the lawn.
Ken:	(*to himself*) Boy, she never gives me help. (*to Charlie*) I thought we were going to play baseball.
Charlie:	Baseball is for kids.
Ken:	Who's a kid?
Mrs. Wagner:	Oh, boy.
Jane:	(*She calls out as she runs next door.*) I'll get the sponges. We can wash your car first and then ours.
	(*Charlie watches her leave and sprays Ken.*)
Ken:	Hey!
Jane:	My father will be happy.
Mrs. Fanelli:	Her father will be very SURPRISED. She never washes the car.

(Charlie stares at Jane and sprays the shutters Mrs. Fanelli is painting.)

Mrs. Fanelli: Charlie, be careful!

Charlie: Sorry.

(Charlie struggles to turn off the hose. Water hits his mother, Mrs. Fanelli, and Ken.)

Mrs. Fanelli: He's watering everything but the lawn. Charlie!

Jane: *(She returns with the sponges.)* Here are the sponges. *(Charlie turns to look at her and hits her with water.)* Ooh!

Mrs. Wagner: Charlie, give me that hose. If ever there was a case of spring fever!

(Charlie finally turns the hose off. The parents laugh. Ken glares. Jane looks surprised.)

A. Answer the questions. Remember to use both short and long answers.

1. What are the signs of spring? → The trees are budding. The grass is growing. The birds are singing.

2. What happened to Mrs. Fanelli's window? → A baseball went through it.

3. Does Mrs. Wagner like spring? → Yes, she does. Mrs. Wagner likes spring.

4. What happened to Mrs. Fanelli's bulbs? → Dogs dug them up.

5. Does Mrs. Fanelli like spring? → No, she doesn't. She doesn't like spring.

6. What does Charlie do all the time? → Daydream. He daydreams all the time.

7. What is Charlie doing now? → Watering the lawn. He's watering the lawn.

8. Is Ken happy? → No, he isn't. He isn't happy.

9. Does Jane ever help Ken? → No, she doesn't. Jane never helps Ken.

10. What does Charlie have? → Spring fever. He has spring fever.

B. Improvise

1. Mr. Wagner comes from behind the house. He finds everyone wet and noisy as they yell at Charlie. What is the conversation?

2. Adam and Jill are friends. They are at the beach. Adam loves sailing and wants to go out in a boat. Jill is disappointed. She wants to swim and sunbathe, but she doesn't want to hurt Adam. What is the conversation?

MAYS
POTATO CHIPS

IN A PICKLE

TRYING TO RECALL; DENYING RESPONSIBILITY

DIRECT AND INDIRECT OBJECTS
WITH AND WITHOUT PREPOSITIONAL PHRASES

Characters: Barbara
Joy
Max } teen-agers
James
Raymond
Evelyn

Scene: A lake miles from town

Barbara: (*folding a blanket*) Where are the keys to the car?

Joy: Max has them. I gave them to him this morning.

Max: I don't have them. I gave you the keys, remember?

Barbara: I gave them back to you.

James: (*He comes from the lake drying his hair with a towel.*) What's wrong?

Max: I gave Barbara the keys and she lost them.

Barbara: I didn't lose them. I gave them to Max.

James: Well, let's find them. We can't stay here. (*He starts looking through the clothing.*)

Joy: Raymond, come help us. (*She starts looking for the keys in the picnic basket.*)

Raymond: Be with you in a minute. (*He is eating potato chips.*)

Max: (*He tries all the doors of the car.*) My father gave me this car with only one set of keys. Raymond!

Raymond: I bet you a dollar they're in your pocket. (*He continues to eat potato chips.*)

Max: I looked in my pocket. (*He looks in his pockets again.*)

99

(Joy and James shake and fold the beach blanket. Max looks under the blanket, Evelyn looks on the ground around the car. Raymond eats.)

Joy: Raymond, give us a hand.

Raymond: Hmm. *(He munches on a sandwich.)*

Evelyn: You gave me the keys, Max, and then I gave them right back to you. Raymond!

Max: I'm going to give him a piece of my mind.

(James tries the car doors again. Max walks down by the lake. Joy and Evelyn sit on the rocks near Raymond. Raymond is eating pickles.)

Joy: Oh, let me have some potato chips, Raymond.

Raymond: Righto. *(He puts his hand into the potato chips to take some for himself. Then he puts his hand in to take some for Evelyn.)*

Evelyn: Give me the bag, Raymond. I can take them myself.

Raymond: Sure. *(He passes the bag after taking another handful of potato chips.)*

Evelyn: *(She puts her hand into the bag. When she pulls it out, she is holding the keys to the car.)* Raymond!

A. Answer the questions. Use both short and long answers.

1. Where are the teen-agers? → At a lake miles from town. The teen-agers are at a lake miles from town.

2. How did they get there? → By car. They got there by car.

3. Whose car did they use? → Max's. They used Max's car.

4. Who looks for the missing keys? → Everyone but Raymond. Everyone but Raymond looks for the missing keys.

5. What does Raymond do? → Eat. Raymond eats while the others look.

6. Who gave Max the car? → His father. His father gave Max the car.

7. Where do they look for the keys? → Everywhere. They look for the keys everywhere.

8. Who finds the keys? → Evelyn. Evelyn finds the keys.

9. Where does she find them? → In the potato chips. She finds them in the potato chips.

10. How did the keys get into the potato chips? → (Students' own answers.)

B. Improvise

1. What is the conversation between Raymond, Max, and Barbara after Evelyn finds the keys?

2. Jason bought a package of cigarettes. He gave the clerk a ten-dollar bill. The clerk gave Jason change for a one-dollar bill. What is the conversation?

WHAT WILL HAPPEN TO THEIR FUTURE?

PUTTING ON AIRS; MAKING PLANS

SIMPLE FUTURE

Characters: Mrs. Harmon
Mrs. Seymour
Mr. Harmon
Mr. Seymour
Arthur Harmon, age nine

Scene: Outside a church on a Sunday morning. The Harmons and the Seymours are next-door neighbors.

Mrs. Harmon: (*after greetings*) Where is your daughter Jean?

Mrs. Seymour: She's on a tour of Europe. She's in Paris right now. Last week she was in Italy, and next week she'll be in Denmark.

Mrs. Harmon: We were in Denmark last year.

Mr. Harmon: And here we are now—at home. What a vacation!

Mrs. Harmon: Never mind, John. Next summer we shall be in Europe again.

Mr. Harmon: No, we won't. You promised me a trip to Japan.

Mrs. Seymour: What will you do with the children?

Mr. Seymour: Will you take them with you?

Mrs. Harmon: No, we'll send them to camp.

Mr. Seymour: Will they be happy there? Won't they miss you?

Mr. Harmon: They'll be happy.

Arthur: I want to go to Japan. (*He pulls on his father's coat sleeve.*)

Mr. Harmon: You'll go to camp.

Arthur:	I'll be unhappy there.
Mr. Harmon:	You won't be unhappy or you'll be sorry.
Mrs. Seymour:	Well, we'll be late for church. Goodbye, Sarah, John.
Mr. Seymour:	Good seeing you, John. Will you be at the club next week?
Mr. Harmon:	I'll be there.
Mr. Seymour:	I'll see you then. Goodbye.
	(*The Seymours walk into church. The Harmons walk slowly behind.*)
Mrs. Harmon:	John, let's take the children to Japan. The trip will be an education.
Mr. Harmon:	Good grief, no! We'll send them to camp. (*He reaches into his pocket for money.*)
Mrs. Harmon:	They won't be happy there.
	(*Arthur listens carefully.*)
Arthur:	I won't be happy.
Mrs. Harmon:	I will speak to your father later, Arthur.
Arthur:	I will be unhappy at camp.
Mrs. Harmon:	"Shall," Arthur. I "shall" be unhappy at camp. (*She puts her hand on Arthur's shoulder.*)
Arthur:	You'll be unhappy at camp?
Mrs. Harmon:	No, Arthur, YOU will be unhappy at camp. I SHALL be unhappy.
Arthur:	I will be unhappy, and you will be unhappy. You'll take me to Japan.
Mrs. Harmon:	No, no, Arthur. I shall . . .
Mr. Harmon:	Good grief, Sarah. You're confusing him. (*He pulls Arthur to his side.*)
Mrs. Harmon:	John, it's important to use correct English. What will happen to the children when they grow up?
Mr. Harmon:	They'll grow up.
Mrs. Harmon:	But what will happen to them?
Mr. Harmon:	They'll survive.
Mrs. Harmon:	But what will happen to their English?
Mr. Harmon:	Their English will be like yours and mine.
Arthur:	Mother, you said "I will speak" to Daddy, but you said "I shall be unhappy." What's the difference?
Mr. Harmon:	There's no difference, Arthur.
Mrs. Harmon:	But John . . .

Mr. Harmon: Arthur, I use "shall" when I write a formal letter. In conversation I avoid the problem and use the contraction.

Mrs. Harmon: John!

Mr. Harmon: Sarah, the only time I hear you use "shall" is when you're with Mrs. Seymour. Now, let's go. We'll miss the sermon!

A. Answer these questions. Remember, when possible use both short and long answers.

1. Are the Seymours and the Harmons neighbors?

   → Yes, they are. The Seymours and the Harmons are next-door neighbors.

2. Where will Jean Seymour be next week?

   → Denmark. She'll be in Denmark.

3. Where will the Harmons be next summer?

   → Japan. They'll be in Japan.

4. Will the Harmons take their children to Japan?

   → No, they won't. They'll send the children to camp.

5. Will Mr. Harmon be at the club next week?

   → Yes, he will. He'll be at the club next week.

6. Will Arthur be happy at camp?

   → No, he won't. He won't be happy at camp.

7. How is Mrs. Harmon confusing Arthur?

   → She is confusing him with the words "will" and "shall."

8. When does Mr. Harmon use "shall"?

   → When he writes a formal letter. Mr. Harmon uses "shall" when he writes a formal letter.

9. How does Mr. Harmon express the future in conversation?

   → He uses contractions. Mr. Harmon expresses the future in conversation by using contractions.

10. When does Mrs. Harmon use "shall"?

    → When she's with Mrs. Seymour. Mrs. Harmon uses "shall" when she's with Mrs. Seymour.

B. Improvise

1. On their way home from church, Mr. and Mrs. Seymour talk about their summer plans. She wants to go to Japan. He wants to go to Latin America. What is the conversation?

2. In Tokyo, Hiroshi, a twenty-year-old student, has told his parents he wants to go to the United States to finish college. They object to the idea. He argues, listing all the things he will do when he gets to the States. What is the conversation?

THE TUTTLES ARE WEARY

ACCUSING; EXPRESSING FATIGUE
REFLEXIVE PRONOUNS

Characters: Mr. Tuttle
Mrs. Tuttle
Ellen, their daughter, age eleven
Peter, their son, age nine

Scene: It is Sunday evening and the Tuttles are sitting on their front porch. Mr. Tuttle is sitting with his eyes closed. Mrs. Tuttle is reading. Their children are playing in the front yard.

Ellen: Mother, Peter tripped me and I hurt myself. (*She runs up to the porch.*)

Peter: (*Peter follows her.*) I did not trip her, Mother. She tripped herself.

Mr. Tuttle: Frances, why can't our children behave themselves?

Ellen: I did not trip myself, Mother. Peter hurt himself and he was angry. Then he tripped me.

Mrs. Tuttle: Ellen, Peter, behave yourselves!

Ellen: Did you hear Mother? You behave yourself!

Peter: YOU behave yourself!

(*They run away.*)

Mr. Tuttle: Other children behave themselves.

Mrs. Tuttle: Ellen and Peter are tired.

Mr. Tuttle: Other tired children behave themselves.

Peter: Dad, Ellen slapped me. (*He runs up to the porch.*)

Ellen: (*She runs up after him.*) He knocked over my bike!

Peter: I did not!

Mr. Tuttle: Did the bike knock itself over? (*He fills his pipe with tobacco.*)

Peter: She knocked it over herself.

Mrs. Tuttle: Behave yourselves or come into the house.

(*The children run away.*)

Mr. Tuttle: Other children enjoy themselves.

(*The Slocum family walks by.*)

Mrs. Tuttle: There go the Slocums.

Mr. Tuttle: The Slocum children behave themselves. (*Ellen and Peter fight again.*) Frances, tomorrow, let's treat ourselves. Let's hire a babysitter and enjoy ourselves downtown—WITHOUT the children.

Mrs. Tuttle: Better yet, let's stay home tomorrow night and hire a babysitter to take the children out.

A. Answer these questions. Remember, when possible use both short and long answers.

1. What are Mr. and Mrs. Tuttle doing?
→ Sitting on their front porch. They're sitting on their front porch.

2. Are the Tuttle children behaving themselves?
→ No, they're not. They're not behaving themselves.

3. Did Ellen trip herself or did Peter trip her?
→ We don't know. We don't know whether Ellen tripped herself or Peter tripped her.

4. Why did Ellen slap Peter?
→ Because she said he knocked her bike over. Ellen slapped Peter because she said he knocked her bike over.

5. Are the Tuttle children enjoying themselves?
→ No, they're not. They're not enjoying themselves.

6. Is Mr. Tuttle happy with his children tonight?
→ No, he isn't. He's weary of the children.

7. Who says the Slocum children behave themselves?
→ Mr. Tuttle. Mr. Tuttle says the Slocum children behave themselves.

8. Is Mrs. Tuttle weary of the children?
→ Yes, she is. She's weary of the children.

9. What does Mr. Tuttle want to do tomorrow? → He wants to treat himself and his wife. He wants to hire a babysitter and go out without the children.

10. What does Mrs. Tuttle suggest? → She suggests that they stay home and hire a babysitter to take the children out.

B. Improvise

1. The next evening Mr. and Mrs. Tuttle are in a restaurant having dinner. They think of the children but remind themselves it is good to be away from the children. What is the conversation?

2. Kathy is leaving for college. She is packing things in a trunk. She bought many new things herself. She received others as gifts. Her mother thinks Kathy is taking too many things to school. What is the conversation?

THANKSGIVING DINNER

EXPRESSING CONFUSION; ANTICIPATING
VERB TENSE REVIEW

Characters: Mr. Taylor   Herman, age seven
Mrs. Taylor   Joel, age ten
Donna, age twelve   Grandfather, Mr. Taylor's father

Scene: The Taylor family is in the kitchen on Thanksgiving morning. They are preparing Thanksgiving dinner.

Mr. Taylor: (*He opens the oven door.*) The turkey's almost done. How are the vegetables?

Mrs. Taylor: (*She looks in at the squash.*) The squash is ready, but I have to mash the potatoes. And peel the onions and . . . (*She takes out a paring knife.*)

Mr. Taylor: I'll prepare the sweet potatoes. (*He gets brown sugar from the cabinet and bumps into Mrs. Taylor.*) Sorry!

Donna: (*She looks into a pot on the stove.*) My cranberries aren't cooking!

Mr. Taylor: What do you mean they're not cooking?

Donna: I put them on an hour ago and they're still raw!

Mr. Taylor: (*He looks under the pot.*) It helps if you turn on the stove.

Donna: Ooh! Will they be ready in time?

Mrs. Taylor: They'll be ready in time. Don't get upset. Whew! It's hot in here. Herman and Joel, what are you doing?

(*The boys are sitting at the kitchen table surrounded by fruit and nuts.*)

Herman: I'm stuffing dates.

Joel: I'm fixing the cornucopia. Let's see—apples, tangerines, grapes, nuts. (*He arranges the fruit in the cornucopia.*)

Herman: Hey, those nuts are for my dates. (*He eats some dates.*)

Mrs. Taylor: Herman, there are plenty of nuts and if you keep on eating dates, you won't be able to eat your dinner.

Herman: Never! I always have room for turkey. (*He puts a date back on the plate.*)

(*Joel eats some grapes.*)

Mrs. Taylor: Joel!

Mr. Taylor: How's the gravy? Don't put too much salt in it.

Mrs. Taylor: (*She is stirring the gravy.*) I always make good gravy. Stop talking and stir. (*She hands him the spoon. Then she takes the turkey from the oven and puts it on the shelf.*) The turkey looks good. Did you make extra stuffing? I don't see it.

Mr. Taylor: Yes, I filled the turkey and then baked a whole dish of extra stuffing. It's on the bottom rack.

Donna: My cranberries aren't cooking! (*She turns and bumps into her mother.*)

Mrs. Taylor: Yes, they are. Be patient and be careful.

Grandfather: (*He comes in with a newspaper.*) Where are the pies? Ah, I see. (*He cuts a piece of pie.*)

Mr. Taylor: Dad! You ate almost a whole pie last night. Leave that alone.

Grandfather: I didn't eat it alone. Joel and Herman helped me. And Donna had some, too. (*He bumps into Mrs. Taylor.*) Oops, sorry.

Mrs. Taylor: It's so hot in here. Boys, stop eating and save your appetites. Grandfather, aren't you watching the football game? Donna, did you set the table?

Donna: It's all ready.

Joel: She set the table, Mom, and didn't leave room for my cornucopia. It's supposed to be in the center of the table. (*Apples fall from the kitchen table.*)

Herman: The turkey goes in the center of the table.

Mr. Taylor: (*He eats a piece of turkey skin.*) The turkey tastes good!

Mrs. Taylor: Why are you touching the turkey now!?

Mr. Taylor: Just testing.

Donna: Can I have the wishbone?

Herman: I want the wishbone.

(*Donna and Herman crowd around the turkey.*)

Mr. Taylor: You can both have the wishbone. Later. (*He takes the stuffing from the oven.*)

Grandfather: That turkey smells so good. (*He reaches for a piece of turkey and bumps into Mrs. Taylor.*)

Mrs. Taylor: Out. Out. Out. Everyone out of this kitchen till I call you for dinner.

Herman: My stuffed dates.

Joel: My cornucopia.

Donna: My cranberries.

Herman: We're helping you, Mom.

Mrs. Taylor: I know you are, Herman. But the best help you can give me is peace and quiet while I organize this meal. Out!

(The children and their grandfather move slowly out of the kitchen. Mr. and Mrs. Taylor turn to the stove.)

A. Answer these questions. Whenever possible use both short and long answers.

1. What day is it?
   → Thanksgiving. It's Thanksgiving.

2. Who's in the kitchen?
   → Everyone. Mr. and Mrs. Taylor, Joel, Herman, Donna, and their grandfather.

3. Who's preparing the sweet potatoes?
   → Mr. Taylor. Mr. Taylor is preparing the sweet potatoes.

4. Who's cooking the cranberries?
   → Donna. Donna is cooking the cranberries.

5. Why aren't the cranberries cooking?
   → Donna forgot to turn the stove on.

6. Who's stuffing dates?
   → Herman. Herman is stuffing dates.

7. Who's fixing the cornucopia?
   → Joel. Joel is fixing the cornucopia.

8. Is the kitchen hot or cold?
   → Hot. The kitchen is hot.

9. Who keeps bumping into Mrs. Taylor?
   → Everyone. Everyone keeps bumping into Mrs. Taylor.

10. What does Mrs. Taylor want?
    → Peace and quiet. Mrs. Taylor wants peace and quiet so that she can organize the meal.

B. Improvise

1. After dinner, Herman and Joel want to play football. Donna wants to visit friends, and Grandfather wants to watch television. Mr. and Mrs. Taylor want help cleaning up. What is the conversation?

2. Leo, Gilbert, Toby, and Helen are preparing a surprise for Ellen's birthday. The four friends are decorating Helen's apartment and arranging food and drinks. They are also selecting music for the party. It's seven thirty in the evening. The party begins at eight. What is the conversation among the group as they rush around the apartment?

BOREDOM

EXPRESSING BOREDOM
GOING-TO FUTURE

Characters: Brian
Doug
David } college students
Marty
Ernest
The waitress

Scene: On a Friday afternoon, Brian, Doug, and David are sitting in a campus snack bar. Doug is drumming his fingers on the table. David is stirring his soda with a straw. Brian is staring out the window.

Brian: What are you going to do tonight, Doug?

Doug: I don't know. What are you going to do? (*He lights a cigarette.*)

Brian: I don't know. (*He turns to David.*) What are YOU going to do?

David: I don't know. Watch television, I guess. (*He turns to Doug.*) What are you going to do?

Doug: Don't know.

(*There is silence again, with drumming and staring. Marty and Ernest enter.*)

Marty: Hi!

Ernest: Hi!

Brian, Doug, David: Hi!

Marty: (*He pulls a chair up to the table.*) What's new?

Doug: Nothing.

(*The waitress comes over.*)

115

Waitress:	May I help you?
Ernest:	A hamburger and a cup of coffee, please.
Waitress:	And you?
Marty:	Just coffee, please.
	(*The waitress leaves.*)
Ernest:	(*speaking to the group*) What are you going to do tonight?
	(*They all shrug.*)
Marty:	George and I are going to play cards.
Doug:	We played cards last night.
Marty:	Oh.
	(*silence*)
David:	There's a dance at the Y.M.C.A.
Brian:	Are they going to have a band?
Ernest:	Are the girls going to go?
David:	Yes.
Marty:	No.
Brian:	Yes? No!? What?
Marty:	Yes, they're going to have a band.
David:	No, the girls aren't going to go.
Doug:	What girls? What girls aren't going to go?
David:	Louise, Clare. Everyone.
Brian:	Why aren't they going to the dance?
David:	They're going to have a party tonight.
Ernest:	A party? They're going to have a party without us?
Marty:	They're giving a party for Vicky. She's going to get married next week. (*There's a long pause.*) It's only for girls.
Ernest, Brian:	Oh.
	(*silence*)
Doug:	What are you going to do tonight, Brian?
Brian:	I don't know.
	(*They all stare—at their drinks and out the window.*)

David: A dance without girls, a party without boys! Good grief! What are you going to do?!

A. Answer these questions. Remember, when possible use both short and long answers.

1. What are Brian, David and Doug doing?
   → Sitting in a campus snack bar. They're sitting in a campus snack bar.

2. Are they active and happy?
   → No, they're not. They're not active and happy. They're bored.

3. What are the boys going to do tonight?
   → They don't know. They don't know what they're going to do.

4. Is there going to be a band at the Y.M.C.A. tonight?
   → Yes, there is. There's going to be a band at the Y.M.C.A. tonight.

5. Are the girls going to go to the dance?
   → No, they're not. They're not going to go to the dance.

6. Why aren't the girls going to go to the dance?
   → Because they're going to have a party. The girls aren't going to go to the dance because they're going to have a party.

7. Who are they going to give the party for?
   → Vicky. They're going to give the party for Vicky.

8. What's Vicky going to do next week?
   → Get married. She's going to get married next week.

9. Why can't the boys go to the party?
   → Because it's only for girls. The boys can't go to the party because it's only for girls.

10. Are the boys going to have an exciting evening?
    → It doesn't look like it.

B. Improvise

1. Louise and Clare come up to the table. What is the conversation?

2. Greg made lasagna for a boy scout troop meeting at his house today, but his sister Teresa and her friends ate the lasagna when he wasn't home. Greg is very angry. What is the conversation between Greg and his sister?

117

STAGE FRIGHT

EXPRESSING FEAR; ENCOURAGING

PRESENT PERFECT

Characters: The director
The stage manager
Mark (Romeo)
Neil, Mark's friend

Scene: Backstage at a theater just before curtain time. The Milwaukee Amateur Dramatic Society is getting ready to put on "Romeo and Juliet." Everybody is ready except for Mark, who is going to play Romeo. Mark enters the dressing room looking sick. His friend, Neil, is with him.

Director: Mark, where have you been? Juliet has been here since six o'clock! Everybody else has been ready for an hour!

Stage Manager: It is now eight o'clock. The play is scheduled to begin at eight o'clock. The rest of the cast has been ready for an hour!

Director: We've looked for you everywhere. Where the blazes have you been?

Mark: I've been everywhere, and I've made a decision. I have come to tell you my decision. I can't act tonight.

Neil: I've been with Mark. He's made a decision. He can't act tonight.

Mark: I've never been on the stage before.

Neil: He's never been on the stage before.

Director: He's never been on the stage before? We've rehearsed this play for six weeks. We've rehearsed this play five nights a week for six weeks, and Mark's been on the stage every single rehearsal!

Mark: I've never been on the stage in front of an audience.

Neil: He's never been on the stage in front of an audience.

Director: (*to Neil*) You've been a great help, haven't you?

Stage Manager:	The lighting man has been ready for an hour. Are we going to put on a play tonight or not?
Director:	Mark's never been in front of an audience before.
Stage Manager:	Oh, that's wonderful! The leading man is nervous. He acted last night. He acted the night before that, and now he's become nervous. Juliet has been here for two hours and now Romeo has arrived nervous.
Mark:	I've forgotten my lines.
Neil:	He's forgotten his lines.
Director:	Who is this person? (*He glares at Neil.*) Mark has never forgotten his lines before. He has not forgotten them now!
Stage Manager:	You've memorized them. You'll remember them.
Mark:	No, no, I won't. I've forgotten my lines. I've forgotten what to do.
Stage Manager:	We've worked on this play for six weeks, Mark. You haven't forgotten your lines. You haven't forgotten what to do!
Mark:	Where's my costume? I've left my costume at home. I can't act without a costume!
Neil:	He's left his costume at home.
Director:	He has not left his costume at home! He left it here last night. Now stop it, Mark, and get ready.
Mark:	(*He struggles with his costume.*) I haven't put on any makeup. I . . .
Stage Manager:	You haven't put on any makeup because you haven't been here. Hold still. (*He begins to put on Mark's makeup.*)
Mark:	Has the audience been there long?
Director:	They've been there for an hour.
Mark:	Tell them I've become sick. I've been in an accident and I've broken my leg.
Neil:	Yes, tell them he's become sick.
Stage Manager:	Neil, I'm going to get the rest of the cast ready. If you haven't gone when I come back, YOU are going to be sick.
Director:	Mark, forget the audience. Pretend it's just another rehearsal. You've done a wonderful job every other time and you'll be fine tonight. You've always wanted to play Romeo. Remember?
Mark:	OK, OK! I'll go on. But I haven't practiced enough. (*He gets ready to stand behind the curtain.*)
Director:	Is everybody ready? Where is Juliet?

Stage Manager: Juliet has just decided that she's not ready. She's never acted in front of an audience and she's forgotten her lines. She hasn't practiced enough.

A. Answer these questions. Remember, when possible use both short and long answers.

1. How long has Juliet been at the theater? → Since six o'clock. She's been at the theater since six o'clock.

2. How long has everybody else been ready? → For an hour. Everybody else has been ready for an hour.

3. Where has Mark been? → Everywhere. He's been everywhere.

4. What has he decided? → That he can't act. He's decided that he can't act.

5. Who has been with Mark? → Neil. Neil has been with Mark.

6. Why has Mark decided that he can't act? → Because he hasn't had enough practice. He's decided that he can't act because he hasn't had enough practice.

7. Has Mark ever forgotten his lines before? → No, he hasn't. He's never forgotten his lines before.

8. Has Neil been helpful? → No, he hasn't. He hasn't been helpful.

9. Has the audience been there long? → Yes, they have. They've been there for an hour.

10. What has Juliet decided? → That she hasn't had enough practice. Juliet's decided that she hasn't had enough practice.

B. Improvise

1. Mark goes to Juliet's dressing room. What is the conversation?

2. Frank and Gloria are brother and sister. They planned to have dinner and go to the movies together after work. Frank has waited for Gloria for thirty minutes. He is angry. Finally she arrives. What is the conversation?